Signs

Symbols

& Omens

About the Author

Raymond Buckland has been interested in the occult and matters metaphysical for over fifty years, has been actively involved in various aspects of the subject for over forty years, and has been writing about it for over thirty years. He has written more than thirty books, has lectured and presented workshops across the United States, and has appeared on major television and radio shows nationally and internationally. He has written screenplays, been a technical advisor for films, and appeared in plays, movies, and videos. Ray comes from an English Romany (Gypsy) family and presently resides, with his wife, Tara, on a small farm in north-central Ohio.

To Write to the Author

If you wish to contact the author or would like more information about this book, please write to the author in care of Llewellyn Worldwide and we will forward your request. Both the author and publisher appreciate hearing from you and learning of your enjoyment of this book and how it has helped you. Llewellyn Worldwide cannot guarantee that every letter written to the author can be answered, but all will be forwarded. Please write to:

Raymond Buckland
℅ Llewellyn Worldwide
P.O. Box 64383, Dept. 0-7387-0234-X
St. Paul, MN 55164-0383, U.S.A.

Please enclose a self-addressed stamped envelope for reply,
or $1.00 to cover costs. If outside U.S.A., enclose
international postal reply coupon.

Many of Llewellyn's authors have websites with additional information and resources. For more information, please visit our website at http://www.llewellyn.com

RAYMOND BUCKLAND

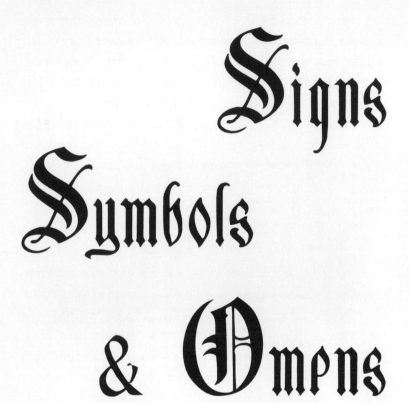

Signs Symbols & Omens

AN ILLUSTRATED GUIDE TO
MAGICAL & SPIRITUAL SYMBOLISM

Llewellyn Publications
St. Paul, Minnesota

First Edition
Third Printing, 2005

Book design by Donna Burch
Cover design by Kevin R. Brown
Editing by Andrea Neff
Interior illustrations © 2003 Raymond Buckland

Library of Congress Cataloging-in-Publication Data

Buckland, Raymond
    Signs, symbols & omens : an illustrated guide to magical & spiritual symbolism/
Raymond Buckland—1st ed.
    p. cm.
Includes bibliographical references.
ISBN 0-7387-0234-X
1. Symbolism. I. Title: Signs, symbols, and omens. II. Title.

BF1623.S9B83 2003
133.3—dc21

                                                                        2003051662

Llewellyn Publications
A Division of Llewellyn Worldwide, Ltd.
P.O. Box 64383, Dept. 0-7387-0234-X
St. Paul, MN 55164-0383, U.S.A.
www.llewellyn.com

Printed in the United States of America

Other Books by Raymond Buckland

Advanced Candle Magic (Llewellyn, 1996)

Amazing Secrets of the Psychic World (Parker, 1975)
  with Hereward Carrington

Anatomy of the Occult (Weiser, 1977)

The Book of African Divination (Inner Traditions, 1992)
  with Kathleen Binger

Buckland's Book of Spirit Communications
  formerly *Doors to Other Worlds* (Llewellyn, 1993, 2003)

Buckland's Complete Book of Witchcraft
  (Llewellyn, 1995)

Buckland Gypsies' Domino Divination Deck
  (Llewellyn, 1986)

Cardinal's Sin (Llewellyn, 1996)

Coin Divination (Llewellyn, 1999)

Color Magick (Llewellyn, 1983 and 2002)

The Committee (Llewellyn, 1993)

Gypsy Dream Dictionary (Llewellyn, 1990, 1998)

Gypsy Witchcraft & Magic (Llewellyn, 1998)

Here is the Occult (HC, 1974)

The Magic of Chant-O-Matics (Parker, 1978)

Mu Revealed (Warner Paperback Library, 1970)
  under the pseudonym "Tony Earll"

A Pocket Guide to the Supernatural (Ace, 1969)

Practical Candleburning Rituals (Llewellyn, 1970, 1976, 1982)

Ray Buckland's Magic Cauldron (Galde Press, 1995)

Scottish Witchcraft (Llewellyn, 1991)

Secrets of Gypsy Fortunetelling (Llewellyn, 1988)

Secrets of Gypsy Love Magic (Llewellyn, 1990)

The Tree: Complete Book of Saxon Witchcraft
   (Weiser, 1974)

Truth About Spirit Communication (Llewellyn, 1995)

Wicca for Life (Citadel, 2001)

The Witch Book (Visible Ink Press, 2002)

Witchcraft Ancient and Modern (HC, 1970)

Witchcraft From the Inside (Llewellyn, 1971, 1975, 1995)

Witchcraft . . . the Religion (Buckland Museum, 1966)

Tarot Kits

The Buckland Romani Tarot (2000)

Gypsy Fortunetelling Tarot Kit (1989, 1998)

Videos

Witchcraft . . . Yesterday and Today (1990)

Acknowlegments

Many thanks to Nancy Mostad, for suggesting this book. Thanks also to Andrea Neff, Donna Burch, Kevin Brown, Hollie Kilroy, and all at Llewellyn for producing this book.

Dedication

To my wife, Tara, who always encourages and supports me.

Contents

INTRODUCTION

The metaphysical field is replete with symbols and sigils, many of them incomprehensible to the uninitiated. In the field of Witchcraft alone there are degree symbols, athame sigils, pentacle signs, and many more. Ceremonial or Ritual Magic contains a host of signs and symbols together with such things as magical alphabets, magic squares, and talisman markings. Voodoo has its vevers, and alchemy possesses another host of symbols. From the well-known zodiacal signs of astrology to the intricacies of the Pennsylvania Dutch hex signs, there are many fascinating secrets to be uncovered.

Speaking of religious symbols, Carl G. Jung said that their role is "to give a meaning to the life of man."[1] Symbols are one thing, but symbolism is much more. Many symbols can be found in various cultures, yet the symbolism of those signs may be very different from one culture to the next. A good example is the swastika. This simple symbol is found as far back as 10,000 B.C.E. The name comes from the Sanskrit, meaning

---

1. Carl G. Jung, *Psychology and Alchemy* (London: Routledge & Kegan Paul, 1953).

"so to be." It is found on ancient Indian coins, on Japanese Buddhas, and in ancient Greece, China, Persia, Scandinavia, and throughout Europe. The Christian Cramponée Cross is a swastika. Frequently the swastika symbolizes the sun. The fact that the Nazis of Germany, in the Second World War, adopted it as their symbol does not make the swastika itself "evil." *No symbol is good or bad in itself; it is what the symbol means to the person using it that is important.* Another example of that is found with the pentagram. An inverted pentagram (with the point downward) is not in itself evil or a symbol of the Christian Devil. The inverted pentagram, again, is found in many places. When used by Satanists it may well be symbolic of evil, yet when used by, for example, Wiccans, it is a symbol of good. So no symbol in and of itself is good or bad. It is how it is used, and how it is regarded by the person(s) using it, that matters.

In this book I try to cover as many signs and symbols as I can in the space available. Obviously it is not possible to cover every single symbol of every country and belief system from all civilizations, but I have tried to include a good representation. I'm sure there will be many I miss and some that belong to the normally hidden inner secrets of various organizations to which I am not privy. Any reader with knowledge of symbols I have neglected, who feels they should be included, please feel free to contact me, care of the publisher, so that we may consider them for inclusion in future editions of this book.

The symbols as I have drawn them are as true as possible to the way they would normally be drawn and used. Some other sources show examples of symbols that are neatly drawn obviously by mechanical means (such as with a compass and straightedge) or that are even computer-generated. I have avoided that and have done virtually everything freehand. The alchemists of old did not use drawing instruments any more than did the Native Americans, the Travelers, the Australian Aboriginals, or most of those from whom I have taken the symbols. So, for the signs and symbols depicted here I have striven for that same "natural" appearance.

—Raymond Buckland

ALCHEMY

Some scholars say the name *alchemy* comes from the Greek *cheo*, meaning "I pour" or "I cast," since much of alchemy has to do with the working of metals. But many believe the word comes from the Egyptian *Khem*, meaning "the black land" (land with black earth), and see that as indicating Egypt as alchemy's place of origin. The Arabic article *al* was added to *Khem* to give *alchemy*. Later, as the science (some call it a pseudoscience) progressed, the article was again dropped, to become *chemistry*. Alchemy certainly is the early history of chemistry.

There was an early Egyptian alchemist whose name was Chemes. He wrote a book, called *Chema*, about his experiments trying to turn base metal into gold. Some few believe that the word alchemist comes from his name.

Whatever the origin of the word, it seems certain that the practice of alchemy had its beginnings in the Hellenistic culture of Alexandria, Egypt, which was the center of the world of learning at that time. In fact alchemy is a blending of Egyptian technology, Greek philosophy, and Middle Eastern mysticism. The first alchemists were the metallurgical workers who prepared precious metals for the nobles but also produced cheap substitutes for the less affluent. These cheaper substitutes were often disguised to look like the more precious metals. It didn't take long for the idea to develop that it might be possible to actually produce the precious metals themselves. This idea, in fact, was backed by Aristotle's theory that there was a prime matter that was the basis for all substances. Astrology added the concept that the greater outer world of planets and stars reflected the inner world of humankind: a macrocosm and a microcosm. It was believed that under the proper astrological influences, it should be possible to change one metal into another; for example, lead into gold. In the same way that humankind perfected, going through death and rebirth, so might metals perfect and grow from one base form to another higher form.

The *Philosopher's Stone* was the term given to a stone that—if it could be developed—would serve as the catalyst to transform metals and other raw material into gold. Although referred to as a stone, it was not necessarily an actual stone for it was believed that it might be a combination of fire and water, or other unlikely mixtures.

So the original alchemy became an operation of passing substances through a series of chemical processes. The actual workings were noted, but in symbolic form to protect them from the dabblers and the uninitiated, and also to protect the alchemists themselves from charges by the Church that they were involved in heresy. The metals were represented by the astrological sign of the controlling body, and frequently the components and the actions were assimilated with Greek and Roman myths and mythological beings. The more the individual alchemists tried to hide and protect the results of their experiments, the more obtuse and confusing became much of what they did and said. In describing necessary actions, they used language such as: "When we marry the crowned king with the red daughter, she will conceive a son in the gentle fire . . . the dragon shuns the light of the sun, and our dead son shall live. The king comes forth from the fire and rejoices in the marriage."[1]

Hermes Trismegistus, also known as "Thrice Great Hermes" (it is from his name that the term *the hermetic art* was given to alchemy), has been variously described as an earthly incarnation of the Egyptian god Thoth and as an Egyptian priest, or a pharaoh, who taught the Egyptians all their magic. He is credited with having written several thousand books, including the Emerald Tablet, or *Tabula Smaragdina*, which contained all the hermetic teachings—the thirteen precepts—including the fundamental principles for the *Grand Arcanum*, or "great secret." There are many references to the Emerald Tablet in alchemical writings.

Instruments

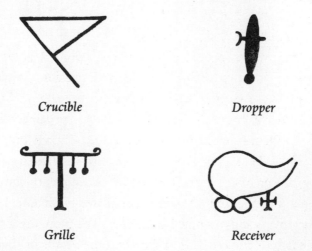

Crucible   Dropper

Grille   Receiver

---

1. *Tractatus aureus* (1610). The *Tractatus aureus* is an alchemical treatise in seven chapters attributed to Hermes Trismegistus.

Instruments *(continued)*

Retort

Scull

Still

Wick

Weights and Measures

Ounce

Dram

Scruple

Pinch

Weights and Measures *(continued)*

Pint

Pound

Spirits

Copper

Mercury

Silver

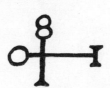

Tin

World of Spirit

Seasons

Spring

Summer

Autumn

Winter

Materials

Gold (i)

Gold (ii)

Gold (iii)

Gold (iv)

Materials *(continued)*

Gold (v)

Gold (vi)

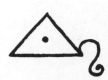

Gold (vii)

Silver (i)

Silver (ii)

Silver (iii)

Alum

Antimony

Materials *(continued)*

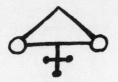

Arsenic-Sulfur

Aqua Vitæ

Bismuth

Borax

Brass

Burned Alum

Burned Hartshorn

Caustic Lime

Materials *(continued)*

Chalc

Cinder

Cinnibar

Clay

Copper

Cribbled Ashes

Crystal

Eggshells

Materials *(continued)*

Ginger

Glass

Gravel

Iron

Iron Filings

Lead

Lime

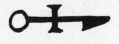

Magnesia

Materials *(continued)*

Manure

Mercury

Nickel

Niter Flowers

Niter Oil

Nitric Acid

Potash

Red Arsenic

Materials *(continued)*

Rock Salt

Sea Salt

Soapstone

Soot

Steel

Stone

Sugar

Sulfur

Materials *(continued)*

Tin

Urine

Verdigris

Vinegar

Vitriol

White Arsenic

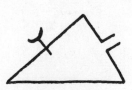

Wine Spirit

Wood

Materials *(continued)*

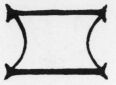

Yellow Arsenic

Yellow Wax

Zinc

Processes

Blackening (melanosis)

Whitening (leucosis)

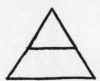

Yellowing (xanthosis)

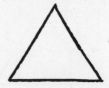

Reddening (iosis)

Processes *(continued)*

Amalgam

Amalgamation

Boil

Compose

Distill

Essence

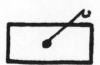

Fumes

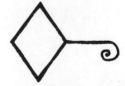

Filter

Processes *(continued)*

Mix

Powder

Purify

Pulverize

Rot

Solve

Sublime

Take

Processes *(continued)*

Torrefaction of Gold

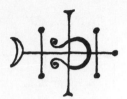

Torrefaction of Silver

Animals, Birds, etc.

Blackbird (blackened mass)

Lion (acid)

Moon/Lunar

Ouroboros (completion)

Animals, Birds, etc. *(continued)*

Stag (soul)

Sun/Sol

Unicorn (spirit)

Birds (volatilization)

Ancient Egypt

During the more than four thousand years that the ancient Egyptian civilization flourished, religion and magic came together as never before . . . nor, perhaps, since. Talismans, amulets, figures, pictures, spells, and formulæ were part and parcel of everyday life. Prayers were intermingled with magical spells, chants, and incantations to protect from the hostile and to encourage the affable. From the earliest pre-dynastic times, the Egyptians saw the whole earth, together with the underworld and the sky above, as home to innumerable invisible beings. Some of these were friendly but many were not. The purpose of the magic that was developed was to give humankind authority over these beings, yet this magic was of both positive and negative kinds. There was magic to benefit the living and the dead, but there was also magic to harm others.

There are numerous papyri containing formulæ for preparing medicine and drugs, such as the Edwin Smith Papyrus (c. 1500 B.C.E.), the Ebers Papyrus, the Hearst Papyrus, and others in both the British Museum and in Turin.[1]

1. See *Life Under the Pharoahs* by Leonard Cottrell (London: Evans Bros., 1955).

Magic certainly played a major role in ancient Egyptian medicine. Despite preparing bodies for embalming (in a formalized, basic operation that never varied), they had little understanding of human anatomy and, hence, little ability to diagnose. The medical panacea to evict evil spirits was magic.

Much, if not most, of ancient Egyptian magic was guided by astrology. Many of the papyri exhort the operator to perform the ritual on a certain day and to avoid days that were thought to be hostile to the act. From these extant writings it is known that the year of the Egyptian calendar was made up of 365 days. Each of those days was divided into three parts, one or two of which were considered lucky or unlucky.

The word *hieroglyph*, from the Greek, means "sacred carvings," and is the word used to describe the numerous carvings and paintings on the walls of the tombs and temples. The Egyptians called these hieroglyphs "the speech of the gods." The symbols themselves were thought to have magical powers. The earliest examples of Egyptian hieroglyphic writing, unlike the picture writing of Native Americans and Eskimos, were made up entirely of pictures that had phonetic values. For example, the horned viper picture became the letter *f*, the cobra the letter *g*, a hand the letter *d*, and an owl the letter *m*. Words were composed by putting together different combinations of symbols. Hieroglyphs were first used about seven thousand years ago and continued in use until about 400 C.E.

It became standard to use certain hieroglyphs by themselves as amulets and talismans. The best known is probably the *ankh*, meaning "life." Others were the tet column ("stability"), the Eye of Horus ("soundness/wholeness"), and sa ("protection").

Most hieroglyphics were colored. Traditional colors were blue for the sky and all celestial objects; red for a human male; yellow or pink-brown for a female; and animals, birds, and reptiles in their natural colors, so far as possible. The "writing" followed a variety of forms. Some hieroglyphics were read from left to right, and some from right to left; some were written in vertical columns, and some in horizontal lines. On either side of a door, for example, the writing would go down each side and would be read from top to bottom. The figures on each side would face in toward each other. In other words, any figures on the left of the door would face to the right, while figures on the right of the door would face to the left. Similarly, the figures on a horizontal line faced the reader. That is, if the figures face to the left, then the writing is read from left to right; if the figures face to the right, then the writing is read from right to left. This is why you may see examples of individual hieroglyphs facing in opposite directions.

There are a tremendous number of hieroglyphs and it is not possible to show them all in a book of this size.[1] Here are the most common ones, including the Egyptian alphabet and some of the determinatives.

Egyptian Alphabet

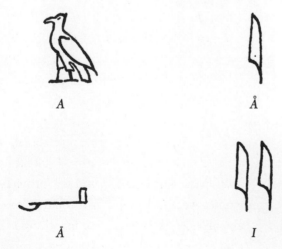

A   Å

Ā   I

1. Recommended is the classic *Egyptian Language* by Sir E. A. Wallis Budge.

Egyptian Alphabet (*continued*)

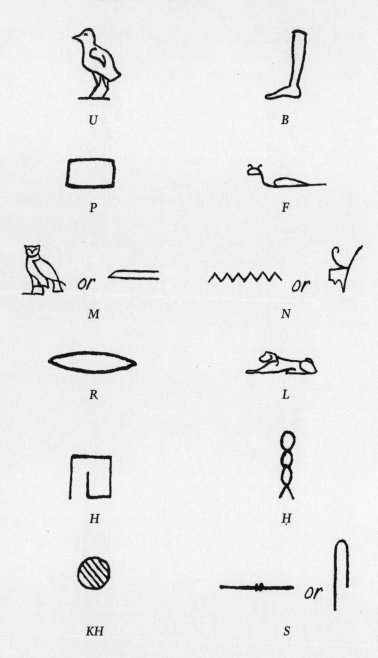

U	B
P	F
M	N
R	L
H	Ḥ
KH	S

Egyptian Alphabet (*continued*)

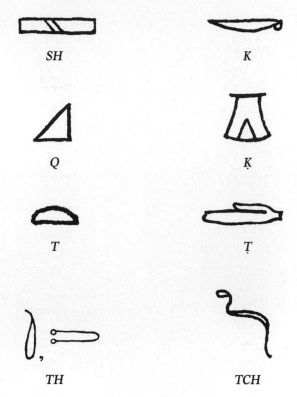

SH	K
Q	Ḳ
T	Ṭ
TH	TCH

Determinatives

God; Divine Being

Goddess

Man

Woman

Tree

Plant; Flower

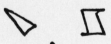

Earth; Land

Road; to travel

Foreign Land

Foreigner

Determinatives *(continued)*

To call or beckon

*To eat; to think; to speak;
whatever done with the mouth*

Inertness; Idleness

Water

House

Animal

Bird

Fish

To cut; to slay

To cook; burn; fire

Determinatives *(continued)*

Smell

To overthrow

Strength

*To walk; to stand;
actions performed with legs*

Flesh

Little; Bad; Evil

Rain; Storm

Day; Time

Village; Town; City

Stone

Determinatives (*continued*)

Metal

Grain

Wood

Wind; Air

Liquid

Crowd

Children

Beard

Right Eye

Left Eye

Determinatives *(continued)*

To see; to look

Right Eye of Ra

Ear

Opening; Mouth; Door

Breast

To embrace

Hand and Arm; to give

Hand

To go; to walk; to stand

Serpent; Body

Determinatives (*continued*)

Worm

Feather

Staircase; to go up

Tet (stability)

Ankh (life)

Magical knot

Rope

Cartouches

For the names of royalty and of deities, the letters are placed in a rectangular frame known as a *cartouche* (so called because it resembles a cartridge). For example, the cartouches for Hatshepset and for Thothmes III would be as follows:

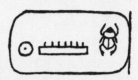

Hatshepset   *Thothmes III*

ASTROLOGY

Originating in Mesopotamia, probably around the third millennium B.C.E., astrology is the art of foretelling events through observation of the planets, fixed stars, sun, and moon, in their juxtaposition and their relationship to the earth. As we know astrology today, it is a combination of the early Babylonian ideas and those of the Egyptians. The Greeks adopted and perfected it, attributing gods and goddesses to the stars and planets. In his *Laws*, Plato proposed a composite god (Apollo-Helios) as the principal deity for the state, uniting the god of mythology with the sun.

An astrological horoscope is, in effect, a diagram of the positions of the planets as seen from a particular spot on the earth at a specific moment in time. The individual's horoscope comes under the heading of *genethliacal* astrology, a branch of *judicial* astrology. Foretelling events of national and international importance is known as *mundane* astrology; answering questions is *horary* astrology; and forecasting weather is *meteorological* astrology.

It is believed that each planet has a particular influence on a person at the time of his or her birth, as well as an influence on the other planets, depending upon their proximity. To draw up, or erect, a chart for an individual, certain things need to be known. The first is the *date* of birth (day, month, year), the second is the *place* of birth (geographical location), and the third is the exact *time* of birth (the hour, to the nearest minute). From these it is possible to determine the exact location of the various stars and planets.

The path of the sun, as seen from the earth, is called the *ecliptic*, and the angle that it makes at any moment, as it rises above the eastern horizon, is the *ascendant*. This name—Ascendant—is also given to the sign of the zodiac that is rising at a given time, with a different ascending sign appearing over the horizon approximately every four minutes. As the sun moves throughout the year, it passes through twelve different areas of sky and constellations. These areas are called *houses* of the zodiac, with the dividing lines between the houses known as *cusps*. The houses each measure thirty degrees, so the sun takes approximately one month to pass through each of the houses. The houses are named as follows:

Aries	March 21 through April 19
Taurus	April 20 through May 19
Gemini	May 20 through June 20
Cancer	June 21 through July 22
Leo	July 23 through August 21
Virgo	August 22 through September 22
Libra	September 23 through October 22
Scorpio	October 23 through November 21

Sagittarius	November 22 through December 21
Capricorn	December 22 through January 20
Aquarius	January 21 through February 19
Pisces	February 20 through March 20

The planets close enough to have an influence on a person are the Sun, Moon (not actually a planet, of course), Mercury, Venus, Mars, Jupiter, Saturn, Uranus, and Pluto. The symbols used in astrology for these planets and for the signs of the zodiac are as follows:

Signs of the Zodiac

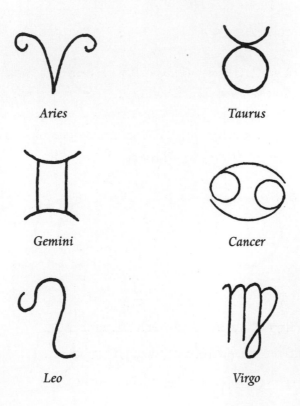

Aries

Taurus

Gemini

Cancer

Leo

Virgo

Signs of the Zodiac *(continued)*

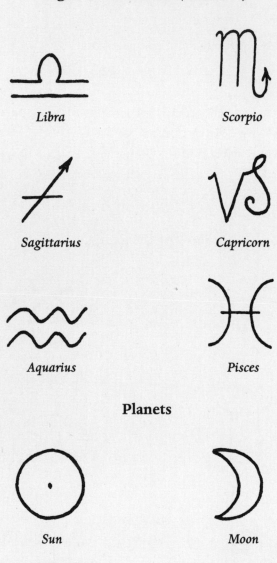

Libra

Scorpio

Sagittarius

Capricorn

Aquarius

Pisces

Planets

Sun

Moon

Mercury

Venus

Planets (*continued*)

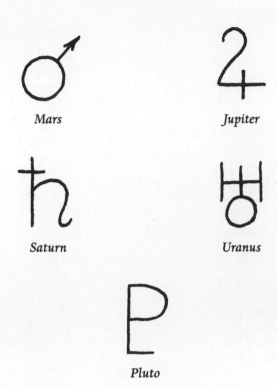

Mars

Jupiter

Saturn

Uranus

Pluto

When considering the relationship of the various planets to each other from the drawn chart, the relative positions are described as *aspects*. They are measured by drawing an imaginary line from the center of the earth to the planets concerned, along the ecliptic (the apparent path of the sun around the earth), and measuring the difference in the angles. Two planets that are 180° apart form an *opposition*. Two planets close together (within 8° to 10° of each other) form a *conjunction*. *Semisextile* is the term for planets 30° apart; *semisquare* (or *semiquartile*) is the term for planets 45° apart; *sextile* for 60°; *quintile* for 72°; *square* (or *quartile*) for 90°; *trine* for 120°; *sesquiquadrate* (or *sesquare*) for 135°, and *quincunx* for 150°. Here are the symbols for the planetary aspects:

Aspects

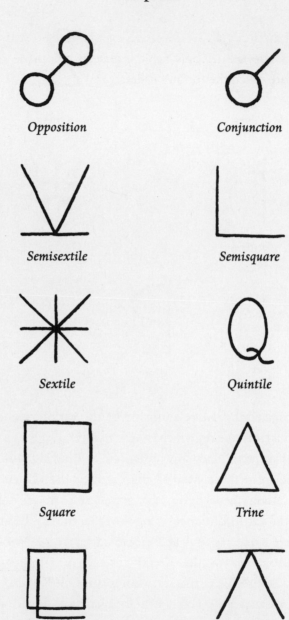

Opposition

Conjunction

Semisextile

Semisquare

Sextile

Quintile

Square

Trine

Sesquiquadrate

Quincunx

The Moon's Nodes

The moon's orbit intersects with the ecliptic (the apparent orbit of the sun around the earth) every nineteen years. The points where the moon's orbit intersects the plane of the ecliptic are called the moon's *nodes*.

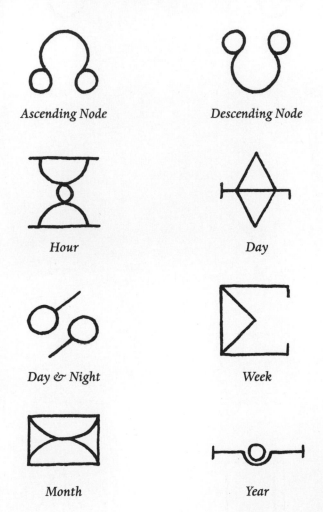

Ascending Node

Descending Node

Hour

Day

Day & Night

Week

Month

Year

Australian Aborigines

Australian Aboriginal art is found mainly as rock engravings, primarily in western New South Wales and northeastern South Australia. Much of it is abstract in form. However, there are also bark paintings and body paintings, plus the decoration of ceremonial objects.

The various tribes have a wide variety of myths featuring, along with humans, such creatures as serpents, turtles and tortoises, jungle fowls, dingos, crocodiles, and other reptiles. Fish and insects are also included. The songs and dances of the rituals frequently enact the adventures of tribal ancestors, and the art complements these songs and dances. The tribal ancestors have become near-gods, who performed miracles and even traveled through the air or under the ground. The myths, chants, and rituals are nurtured in secret mystical lodges to which the men of the tribe belong. The men decide when, or even if, to pass on their knowledge to the younger men.

In the north of the Northern Territory, women play a more important role than elsewhere. It is there that can be found the myth of the Great Fertility Mother. It was she who first arrived, from the sea, and gave birth to humans as she moved from place to place. The Rainbow Snake, a python, also plays an important role in this area. He is associated with the rains and floods; with the wet season.

The Aborigines believe in reincarnation and in the transmigration of souls into animals and reptiles. Death is accepted, since all will be reborn.

Rainbow Serpent

This is the Rainbow Serpent of Energy; the sacred body of the earth and spiritual order of the universe. Serpents are featured a lot in Aboriginal art. The Rainbow Serpent is the unity between the physical and the spiritual worlds. It is believed to be attracted to rituals in which the participants are painted in red ochre, which, in turn, increases the sexual energy of the ritualists.

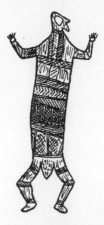

Mungada

This is the medicine man, Mungada, who cures the sick. He does not practice black magic and is not feared. However, his pictorial form is very similar to that of Gurumuka, the night-dwelling spirit who is greatly feared. The differences are in the decorations: the bands of color around the arms, legs, and face. Gurumuka also has large teeth sticking out with which he bites his victims.

Gundaman

Here is the Gundaman lizard. As with many Aboriginal paintings, this reptile is drawn in what amounts to an x-ray view, showing internal organs (in this case the lungs and alimentary canal).

Laitjun

Laitjun was a mythical figure in the Blue Mud Bay area of Arnhem Land. He was the son, or a second aspect, of the god Banaitja. Laitjun showed the Aborigines what designs they should paint on their bodies.

Big-Breasted Women

The cave paintings found at Unbalanja Hill, Arnhem Land, include many figures of women. A number of these, for whatever reason, are depicted with very large breasts. They have become known as the "Big-Breasted Women."

Aztec and Mayan

The Aztecs and the Mayans have been compared to the Romans and the Greeks. The Aztecs, like the Romans, were warlike, building on the ruins of those they conquered. They also organized and developed government. Like the Greeks, the Mayans were an intellectual, artistic people. They developed architecture, sculpture, painting, and even astronomy.

Aztecs

The Aztecs were not fully established until 1325 C.E., at which time they obtained their freedom from the king of Colhuacan, who had held them in servitude. They found a place that fulfilled a prophecy and there established their main city of Tenochtitlan (what was later to grow into Mexico City).

The Aztecs believed in a world with gods of nature, but with a supreme deity. In Wicca, and other religions, male and female are seen throughout nature as necessary for life. This led to the belief that there must also be male and female with the gods. In similar fashion, the Aztecs saw their supreme power as being both male and female. This deity was named Ometecuhtli (also sometimes known as Tloque Nahuaque), which means "Two-Lord." Sometimes figures of Ometecuhtli show a hermaphroditic figure. He is the original bestower of all life and was addressed in religious poems as "Cause of All." He dwells in the highest heaven. Beneath him are found, in order, the Place of the Red God of Fire, the Place of the Yellow Sun God, and the Place of the White Evening Star God. The oldest of the gods, however, was Ueueteotl (meaning "old, old, god"), whose place of honor was the fireplace in every homestead.

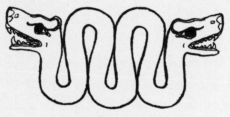

Double-Headed Serpent

The double-headed serpent was a popular image associated with life-giving rain. It was part of the rites of Tlaloc, god of the mountains, rain, and springs.

Tlaloc

Tlacolteutl

Tlacolteutl, an earth and fertility goddess, is represented here much like a European witch, riding astride a broomstick. She holds a serpent, which is red—the Aztec symbolic color for sex.

Precious Metals

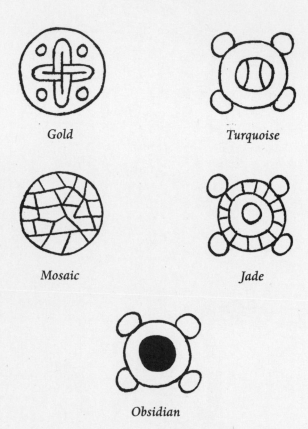

Gold

Turquoise

Mosaic

Jade

Obsidian

Place names often incorporate hieroglyphs for local vegetation, and city names may include the time of year, or even the day, the town was founded. The following symbols are the names of some Aztecan places. The series of rectangles on the first, Caltepec, which may also be seen within the last, Tecalco, is the hieroglyph for a house *(calli)*. What looks like a pair of animal feet, in Miztlan, Itztlan, and Petlatlan, is the hieroglyph for teeth *(tlan)*.

Names of Aztecan Places

Caltepec

Itztepec

Atepec

Pantepec

Miztlan

Itztlan

Petlatlan

Tecalco

The Twenty Days of the Month
on the Aztecan Calendar

Crocodile (Cipactli)

Wind (Ehecatl)

House or Temple (Calli)

Lizard (Cuezpallin)

Snake (Coatl)

Death (Miquiztli)

Deer (Mazatl)

Rabbit (Tochtli)

The Twenty Days of the Month
on the Aztecan Calendar *(continued)*

Water (Atl)

Dog (Itzcuintli)

Monkey (Ozomatli)

Herb (Malinalli)

Reed (Acatl)

Jaguar (Ocelotl)

Eagle (Quauhtli)

Vulture (Cozcaquauhtli)

The Twenty Days of the Month
on the Aztecan Calendar *(continued)*

Movement (Olin)

Stone (Tecpatl)

Rain (Quiahiutl)

Flower (Xochitl)

Here are the symbols for specific years, or "year bearers": Wind year; Deer year; Herb year; Movement year. Since there are no month signs recorded, the small circles indicate the number of times in the year that the particular day has appeared; for example, the eleventh occurrence of the day in that year.

Year Symbol

Specific Years

Wind Year

Deer Year

Herb Year

Movement Year

Mayans

The Mayan Indians developed in the humid lowlands of Central America, especially in the Yucatan Peninsula. They predate the Aztecs by almost 2,000 years, having their calendar system working as early as 600 B.C.E. Their most brilliant period was from 300 to 900 B.C.E., generally known as the Maya Golden Age. This time period covered the most sophisticated calendrical observations utilizing a 260-day almanac in conjunction with a 365-day calendar.

Mayan art was superior to Egyptian art (for example, in their drawing of the human figure), because the Mayans could draw the human figure in front view and pure profile without distortion. Yet humans were seldom dealt with in Mayan art, since the gods were not in human form. At best they were half human and half animal. Most common was a serpent motif, though that was seldom represented realistically. Parts of other creatures might be added to a serpent, with scrolls and other elaborate details added. For example, sometimes a human head would be placed in the serpent's distended jaws.

Representations of the Moon

Sun and Moon Hieroglyph

Moon, as depicted in a "celestial band"

The Four Directions

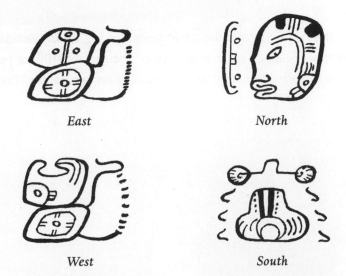

East   North

West   South

Face Numerals

Here are some examples of face numerals found in Mayan inscriptions. In most cases, these are the faces of gods.

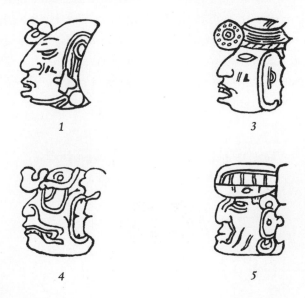

1   3

4   5

Face numerals *(continued)*

6   9

10

It seems likely that the Mayans first had a lunar-solar calendar of twelve months of thirty days each. Later they reduced the number of days in a month to twenty, and increased the number of months to eighteen. Then an extra five-day month was added to make 365 days. The extra quarter-day per year was understood but not worked into the calendar.

Here are the nineteen month signs (eighteen plus *Uayeb*, the five-day month), as given both in the inscriptions and in the codices.

The 19 Month Signs, as Given in the Mayan Inscriptions

Pop

Uo

The 19 Month Signs, as Given in the
Mayan Inscriptions *(continued)*

Zip

Zotz

Tzec

Xul

Yaxkin

Mol

Chen

Yax

The 19 Month Signs, as Given in the Mayan Inscriptions *(continued)*

Zac

Ceh

Mac

Kankin

Muan

Pax

Kayab

Cumhu

The 19 Month Signs, as Given in the
Mayan Inscriptions *(continued)*

Uayeb

Zero

The 19 Month Signs, as Given in the
Mayan Codices

Pop

Uo

Zip

Zotz

Tzec

Xul

The 19 Month Signs, as Given in the
Mayan Codices *(continued)*

Yaxkin

Mol

Chen

Yax

Zac

Ceh

Mac

Kankin

The 19 Month Signs, as Given in the Mayan Codices *(continued)*

Muan

Pax

Kayab

Cumhu

Uayeb

Zero

ℬUDDHIST

Gautama Siddhartha (c. 563–483 B.C.E.) was a young prince of northeast India who suddenly, at age twenty-nine, discovered the pain and suffering that existed in the world. Up until that time his father had sheltered him from all contact with anything but pleasure and luxury (his mother had died shortly after his birth). Siddhartha was born among the Sakyas, a tribe of the Kshatriya warrior caste in what is now Nepal. His father ruled the Gautama clan, and in later years Siddhartha himself became known as Gautama, though it was not his given name.

Upon his "rude awakening," Siddhartha renounced his home and family and set out to seek the "supreme peace of Nirvana." He was taught by two Brahmin religious teachers, but, unsatisfied, he looked elsewhere. After trying many practices, including extreme asceticism, he finally found what he was looking for through meditation. It is said that it came to him as he sat under a boddhi tree, or Tree of Wisdom. He determined

that the cause of all the suffering in the world, and of the end-
less series of birth and rebirth, was what he saw as selfish
craving or desire. If this can be extinguished, there can be
freedom from the Wheel of Life and the never-ending suffering associated with it. In discovering this, Siddhartha became
Buddha, or "the Enlightened One." For the next forty-five years
he wandered the country teaching what he had learned. He organized a community of monks, known as the *sangha*, to con-
tinue his teachings after his death. They preached "The Word,"
known as the *Dharma*.

Buddha's simple formula is: "I take refuge in the Buddha; I
take refuge in the Dharma; I take refuge in the Sangha" . . . the
Buddha, the Teaching, and the Order. There is no priesthood
and there are no other rites or creeds. All that the teacher can
do is set the listener on the path by example and precept. It
was not until sixty years after his death that Buddha's teachings
were set down in writing. These teachings became known as
the *Sutras* (from the Sanskrit meaning "thread").

Buddha's enlightenment consisted of the realization of four
basic truths, usually referred to as the *Four Noble Truths*: Life en-
tails dissatisfaction (pain); dissatisfaction is a result of clinging
and craving; there's an end to all dissatisfaction; the way to the
end of dissatisfaction is the path. In turn, "the Path," or the
Eightfold Path, is wisdom (right view, right thought), morality
(right speech, right action, right livelihood), and meditation
(right effort, right mindfulness, right concentration).

Buddhism is today the religion of Burma, Thailand (Siam),
Cambodia, Laos, Sri Lanka (Ceylon), Tibet, half of Japan,
much of China, and is found in many other countries around
the world. It has a large following in the United States, where
there are now more Buddhists than can be found in India.

Mandala

Aids to meditation, and in particular to Tantric meditation, are known as *mandalas*, a Sanskrit word meaning "circle." The word is used in Hindu and Buddhist ritualism to denote a mystical diagram. It is one of the most widespread of all symbols, with hundreds of variations. Many are composed of a circle enclosing a square with a central symbol. A mandala is also the enclosure of sacred space—*imago mundi*—much like a ceremonial magician's magic circle.

The mandala shown here is known as the *Sri Yantra*, or "Great" Yantra. It is made up of interlocking triangles surrounded by an eight-petal and a sixteen-petal lotus, with the border symbolizing the four directions. The whole is a mystical representation of the creative process.

Daiji (Yin-Yang)

The Daiji, or yin-yang, is the symbol of Samsara (the cycle of rebirth) and Nirvana. It was originally a Chinese symbol of opposites.

Triratna

The Triratna is the symbol for the "Three Jewels" of Buddha, Dharma, and Sangha.

Naga

Naga is the protector of Buddha's law.

Swastikas

The swastika is a symbol of Buddha's law and a sign of good fortune.

Shrivasta

With no beginning, middle, or end, this infinite knot is symbolic of long life and love. The Shrivasta is a common symbol in Tibetan Buddhism. It harmoniously weaves simplicity and profundity, motion and rest. Like Buddha's knowledge, it is infinite.

Dharmachakra

The Dharmachakra symbolizes the Wheel of the Law, the eight spokes representing the Eightfold Path.

Buddha's Footprint

Here is the Buddha's Footprint, which includes the swastika, mace, fish, vase, conch shell, and the Wheel of the Law. There is a parallel with the "Footprint of Vishnu." Many ancient peoples felt that it was necessary to stand barefoot on holy ground in order to absorb the sacred energies there.

Trisula

The Trisula is sometimes referred to as Buddha's monogram, other times as a symbol of the Dharma. Indian worshippers of the god Shiva look upon it as the symbol of Shiva's trident.

ℭELTIC

Celt, or Kelt, is from *Keltoi*, the Greek word (from at least the sixth century B.C.E.) for the Pagan people who were spread across Europe and the Iberian Peninsula. In Latin it became *Celtæ*. Spreading across the English Channel and the Irish Sea, these people took root in the British Isles. The Celts had a rigidly structured social and religious organization, the latter administered by their priesthood, the Druids.

The Celts were basically farmers and cattle herders. They were also great hunters and they enjoyed physical combat. They would steal one another's cattle and fight at the slightest provocation. The gods they worshipped were offered—among other things—the heads of the Celts' enemies. They were, in effect, headhunters. Along with the main deities they worshipped, the Celts also acknowledged a whole host of minor spirits, demons, and fabulous creatures. Some of these, they believed, could change shape at will. Although they built no formal temples, the Celts did have sanctuaries that were clearly defined, often utilizing natural features of the land, such as hills, valleys, springs, and groves of trees.

The Celts lived in tribes and it was to the individual tribe that allegiance was sworn. They had no written language, yet they influenced the art of Britain, and especially of Ireland. Medieval Irish monks wrote of the Celts with greater accuracy than did the classical Greeks and Romans, and their heritage lives on in Ireland.

The Celts brought the knowledge of iron to Western Europe and helped spread that knowledge, inventing iron plowshares, scythes, and even primitive reaping machines. They were the first to put iron rims on the wheels of their carts and chariots. Although they never developed a written language, and built no great cities, the Celts left a legacy including artwork in stone, iron, bronze, pottery, gold, and precious metals.

St. Magnus Cross

The St. Magnus cross is a Celtic design that was found carved into the stonework below the large East Window of St. Magnus Cathedral, in the Orkneys, Scotland. Construction of the cathedral began in 1137 C.E., by Earl Rognvald Brusison.

Celtic Knots

Celtic Knots

Celtic knots, as an imitation of basketry, plaiting, and weaving, were used for decoration on stone and wood, and on jewelry. Some exquisite knotwork may be seen in some of Ireland's treasured masterpieces such as the gold-trimmed silver Ardagh chalice and the Tara brooch. This knotwork was later also picked up in manuscripts written by Christian priests. In the latter, for example, the elaborate interlacing was often used on initial letters and elsewhere, sometimes incorporating figures of humans, animals, and reptiles. Although similar interlacing borders and panels can be found in the art around the Mediterranean area, those of the Pictish school of Celtic art seem to be the most elaborate.

Green Man

Also known, variously, as Jack of the Green, Robin o' the Woods, and as a foliate mask (from the makeup of foliage), the Green Man was a representation of the god of the Old Religion, in his aspect of God of Nature. By this time the horns or antlers of the hunting god had given way to the branches and leaves of nature.

Four-Leaf Clover

Since they are so rare, it is believed that to find a four-leaf clover is to have good luck (and to carry it is to retain that good luck). The four leaves are said to represent love, health, wealth, and fame.

Mandrake

The mandrake root (*Atropa mandragora*) grows naturally in the shape of a human being. Because of this it was once believed to have great magical properties and would fetch a high price when sold. The more it looked like a human being, the higher was the price that could be obtained. Because of this, many magicians were not averse to modifying the plant as it grew. They would find a young mandrake and carefully dig it up. Examining it, they would cut away small pieces to make it look more human, even carving a face into it if necessary. They would then place it back in the earth and let it grow for another month or so. Again they would carefully dig it up and examine it. And again they might modify it before putting it back. By the time the mandrake was fully grown, when dug up it looked as though it had grown naturally looking exactly like a human being, and so it could be sold for a very high price.

CEREMONIAL MAGIC

Toward the end of the Middle Ages, many of the more learned, and moneyed, occultists indulged in Ceremonial Magic. The higher dignitaries of the Church were especially attracted to it, having the time, the finances, and the knowledge to practice. Although this form of magic involved the conjuring of entities—also known, variously, as demons and spirits—the practice was not frowned upon by the Church, nor considered heresy, since it was not a religion but merely a practice.

The object of the practice was to use powerful conjurations to force a variety of spirits to appear before the magician, thus showing his (or her) power over them. Having established that superior force, the magician could then order the entity to do whatever he demanded. Apparently capable magicians such as Johann Wierius (also known as John Wier), a Roman Catholic, and the Frenchman Fromenteau, working over many years in the sixteenth century, determined exactly how many demons there were. Wierius said there were no less than 7,405,926 such demons, organized into 1,111 divisions of 6,666 each, together with 79 princes. During the Reformation, Wierius' figures were "corrected" by the Lutherans to 2,665,866,746,664 demons!

Each of these entities was given a name and was recognized as having a particular field of influence. For example, Agares, a duke, could stop movement and could also bestow the gift of languages. Cimeries, a marquis, taught grammar and logic and was able to locate buried treasure. Furcas, another duke, taught philosophy, astronomy, and other sciences. Saleos was able to promote love between the sexes.

The conjuration was elaborate. First of all, the tools used had to be carefully made by the magician, following traditional formulæ. Materials included virgin parchment, gold, silver, the finest river sand, certain woods cut from trees at specified hours, silk garments woven by a young virgin, and so on. Each and every one of these objects had to be consecrated before use, again according to a certain formula. All the necessary information was kept by the magician in a large, handwritten volume known as a *grimoire* (from the Old French for "grammar"). Some of the most famous grimoires were *The Greater Key of Solomon*, *The Lesser Key of Solomon*, *The Calvicle*, *The Grimoire of Honorius the Great*, *The Lemegeton (or "The Book of the Spirits")*, *The Heptameron*, *The Almadel*, *The Pansophy of Rudolph the Magus*, *The Book of Sacred Magic of Abra-Melin the Mage*, *The Black Pullet*, and *Le Dragon Rouge*. These books were jealously guarded by their creators, who frequently wrote passages in code so that the secrets could not be discovered and used frivolously by one not of the Brotherhood. The codes (actually letter substitutions) were known as *magical alphabets*, the best known being Theban, Malachim, Passing the River, and Angelic. Later, Egyptian hieroglyphs, runes of various types, and other writings were also used. (See also the chapter on Magical Alphabets.)

The tools of Ceremonial Magic were many and specific. There were wands, rods, batons, tridents, swords, knives, goblets, bells, cloths, robes, crowns, and even special pens and inks. Rituals were performed in intricate magic circles, constructed to protect the magician from the wrath of the conjured spirit, who was angry at having been summoned. Talismans of protection were also made and worn by the magician. Some of these simply bore what were considered "Words of Power" (the names of the angels and archangels, for example), while others were covered with magical squares, signs, and sigils, all designed to protect. There were a great many symbols used, often made up by the particular magician for a specific conjuration. Here are some of the more common ones, though they varied from grimoire to grimoire.

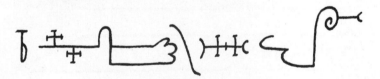

Symbols for marking the magician's robes

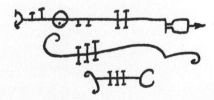

Symbols for marking the assistant's (disciple's) garments

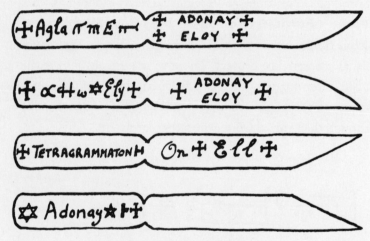

Symbols for marking the crowns of the assistants

Symbols for marking the sword

Sirdar Ikbal Ali Shah, in his book *Occultism: Its Theory and Practice*, gives four illustrations for the sword; the obverse and reverse of two different swords. Where he gives the names Adonay, Eloy, and Tetragrammaton, these would actually have been inscribed using Hebrew characters.

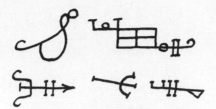

Symbols for marking the shoes

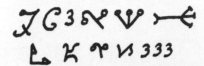

Symbols for marking the knife with a white hilt

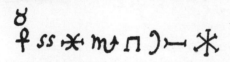

Symbols for marking the knife with a black hilt

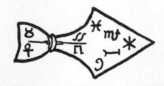

Symbols for marking the scimitar

Symbols for marking the short lance

Symbols for marking the dagger and the poniard

Symbols for marking the burin

Symbols for marking the bell

Symbols for marking the wand and staff

Symbols for marking the trumpet

Symbols for marking the silken cloth

Symbols for marking the necromantic trident

Symbols for marking the baton

Symbols for marking the baguette

Symbols for marking the virgin parchment

Symbols for marking the magic candle

The Magic Seals of the Seven Angels
of the Seven Days of the Week

Michael (Sunday)

Gabriel (Monday)

Samael (Tuesday)

Raphaël (Wednesday)

The Magic Seals of the Seven Angels
of the Seven Days of the Week *(continued)*

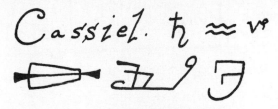

Sachiel (Thursday)

Anaël (Friday)

Cassiel (Saturday)

Signs and Seals of the Demons and Spirits

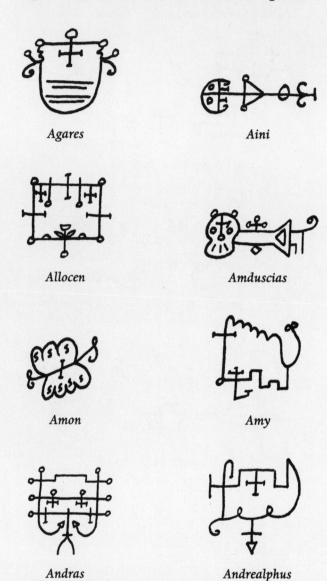

Agares

Aini

Allocen

Amduscias

Amon

Amy

Andras

Andrealphus

Signs and Seals of the Demons and Spirits *(continued)*

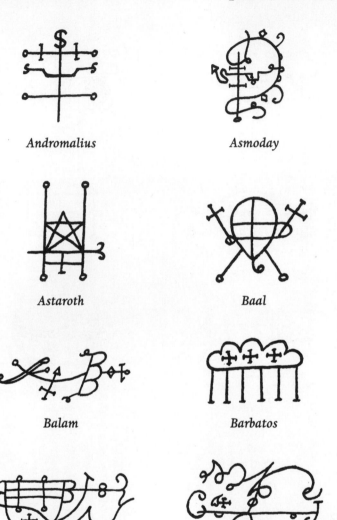

Andromalius

Asmoday

Astaroth

Baal

Balam

Barbatos

Bathin

Beleth

Signs and Seals of the Demons and Spirits *(continued)*

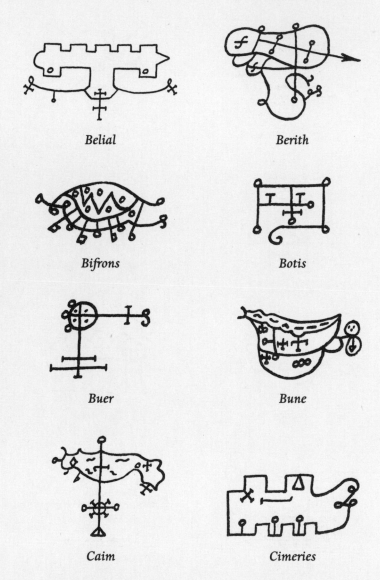

Belial

Berith

Bifrons

Botis

Buer

Bune

Caim

Cimeries

Signs and Seals of the Demons and Spirits *(continued)*

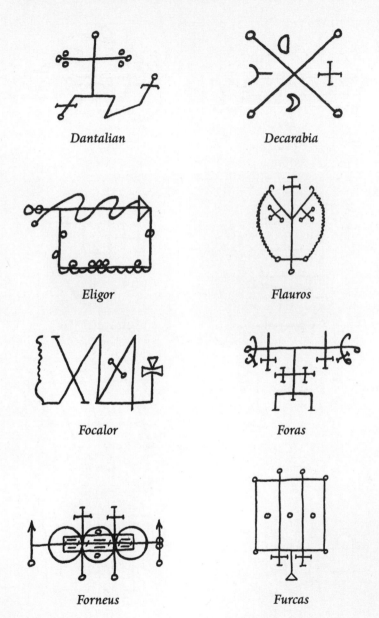

Dantalian

Decarabia

Eligor

Flauros

Focalor

Foras

Forneus

Furcas

Signs and Seals of the Demons and Spirits (continued)

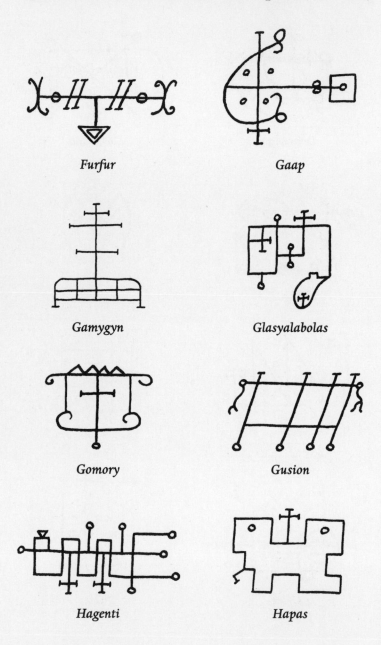

Furfur

Gaap

Gamygyn

Glasyalabolas

Gomory

Gusion

Hagenti

Hapas

Signs and Seals of the Demons and Spirits *(continued)*

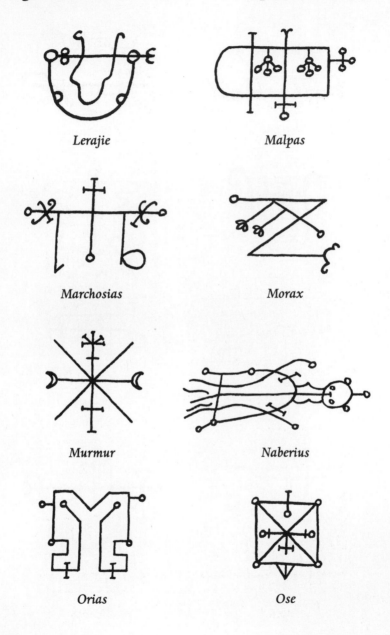

Lerajie

Malpas

Marchosias

Morax

Murmur

Naberius

Orias

Ose

Signs and Seals of the Demons and Spirits *(continued)*

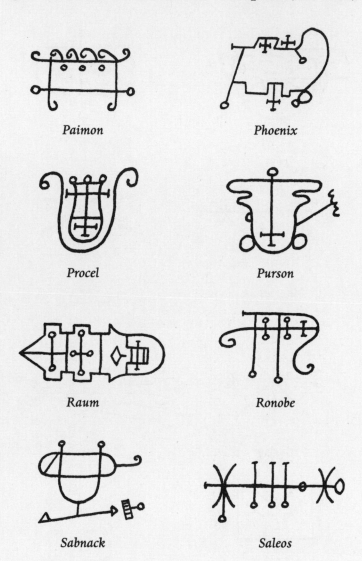

Paimon

Phoenix

Procel

Purson

Raum

Ronobe

Sabnack

Saleos

Signs and Seals of the Demons and Spirits *(continued)*

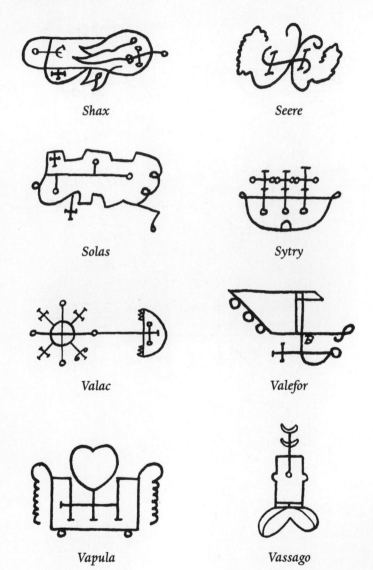

Shax

Seere

Solas

Sytry

Valac

Valefor

Vapula

Vassago

Signs and Seals of the Demons and Spirits *(continued)*

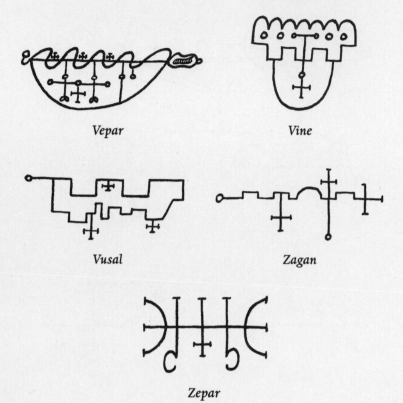

Vepar   Vine

Vusal   Zagan

Zepar

The Magic Seals of the Three Princes
of the World of Spirits

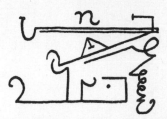

Prince Almishak

Prince Amabosar

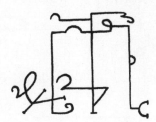

Prince Ashirikas

Symbols for the Seals of the Planets and for Their Spirits and Intelligences

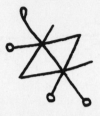

Seal of Saturn

Intelligence of Saturn

Spirit of Saturn

Seal of Jupiter

Intelligence of Jupiter

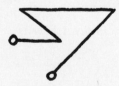

Spirit of Jupiter

Symbols for the Seals of the Planets and for Their Spirits and Intelligences *(continued)*

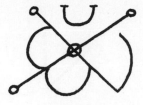

Seal of Mars

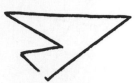

Intelligence of Mars

Spirit of Mars

Seal of the Sun

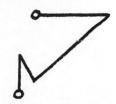

Intelligence of the Sun

Spirit of the Sun

Symbols for the Seals of the Planets and for Their Spirits and Intelligences *(continued)*

Seal of Venus

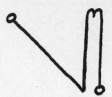

Intelligence of Venus

Spirit of Venus

Seal of the Moon

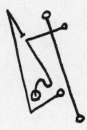

Intelligence of the Moon

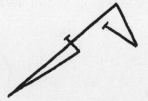

Spirit of the Moon

Symbols for the Seals of the Planets and for Their Spirits and Intelligences *(continued)*

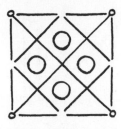

Seal of Mercury

Intelligence of Mercury

Spirit of Mercury

Various magicians used a variety of small circles drawn on the ground, into which they would conjure the summoned spirit; but, with so many hundreds of thousands of different spirits, these are too numerous to include in a book of this size. Please see the Bibliography for more detailed books on this subject.

Sigils for the "Characters of Good Spirits" and "Characters of Evil Spirits" were given in some grimoires.

Characters of Good Spirits

A Simple Point

Round

Characters of Good Spirits *(continued)*

Starry

Perpendicular

Horizontal

Oblique

Bowed Line

Waving Line

Toothed

Intersection Right

Inherent

Adherent Separate

Characters of Good Spirits *(continued)*

Oblique Intersection Simple

Mixed

Manifold

Perpendicular Right Dexter

Sinister

Neuter

Whole Figure

Broken

Characters of Good Spirits *(continued)*

Half

A Letter Inhering

A Letter Adhering

Separate Letter

Characters of Evil Spirits

Right Line

Crooked

Reflexed

A Simpler Figure

Penetrate

Broken

Characters of Evil Spirits *(continued)*

R

A Right Letter

Я

Retrograde

Ƀ

Inversed

Flame

Wind

Water

Flying Thing

Creeping Thing

Serpent

Eye

Characters of Evil Spirits *(continued)*

Hand

Foot

Crown

Crest

Horns

Scepter

Sword

Scourge

CHINESE

The three main religions of China are Buddhism (see the chapter on Buddhist symbols), Confucianism, and Taoism. Confucius is the Latinized form of K'ung Ch'iu. He was a man born in 551 B.C.E., in what is now the province of Shantung. He was a contemporary of Buddha and died in 479 B.C.E. He was a great teacher, traveled a lot, and was instrumental in collecting together the Chinese classical writings that became the basis of a religious movement named after him. Taoism is attributed to Lao Tse, who was born before K'ung Ch'iu, in 604 B.C.E. He was the author of a book known as the *Tao Te Ching*, or *Book of the Way*, which seeks to discover unchanging reality and preaches humility and pacifism.

Many of the Chinese symbols are found in the tools of *Feng Shui* (pronounced "Fung Shway"): the arrangement of things for the greatest harmony. Others, such as the pictogram for the sky, are more general symbols.

Shou (symbol of long life)

Chinese script symbol for the sky

Ch'i (living energy)

Yin

Yang

Pa Kua of the Later Heaven

Double Wheel, representing infinity; earth's eternal cycles of life

The Five Elements

Earth Element

Fire Element

Metal Element

Water Element

Wood Element

The Four Celestial Animals

Green Dragon (abundance and prosperity)

White Tiger (protection)

Crimson Phoenix (opportunity)

The Four Celestial Animals *(continued)*

Black Turtle (support)

CHRISTIAN

Christianity appears in a wide variety of forms, perhaps the most prominent today being Roman Catholicism and Protestantism. At its inception, Christianity was an amalgam of Judaism and the Graeco-Roman religion, taking its name from Jesus of Nazareth who was regarded by some as the "Chosen One," or "Anointed One"; the *Christ*, of God (from the Greek *Christos*).

As the Christian Church has grown and spread over the past two thousand years, it has incorporated a vast number of symbols, some of which have, like many other aspects of the religion, been adopted from earlier Pagan uses. The most prominent symbol is the cross. Although devout Christians revere the cross, most are unaware that it is actually an ancient symbol that has long been venerated by a wide variety of Pagans. Early examples of crosses were used by the ancient Assyrians and the Sumerians. Most such early examples were equal-armed crosses and represented the sun. Equal-armed crosses within circles similarly represented the sun. The cross can also be seen to represent the four seasons, though this would seem to be a later symbolism. A variation of the cross is the swastika (also known as the gammadion, the tetraskelion, the fylfot, and the cross cramponnée), a cross with extended, bent arms.

The cross was not used openly as a symbol of Christianity until the fourth century c.e., by which time the faith had become the official religion of the Roman Empire. In medieval art, the cross on which Jesus was crucified is often depicted as a tree. The most common form of the cross—with the extended lower leg—is known as the *crux capitata*. The cross has also been shown to be T-shaped (the *crux commissa*) or even X-shaped (the *crux decussata*).

The fifth century brought a popular form of the cross known as the *monogrammatic cross*, since it was a modification of a monogram made up of the two Greek letters *Chi* and *Rho*, the first two letters of *Christos*.

One form of the cross has two cross pieces. The second, smaller piece symbolizes the scroll bearing Jesus' name that was nailed to the cross of crucifixion. Occasionally a third, even smaller cross piece is added to represent the foot board.

Crosses and Variations

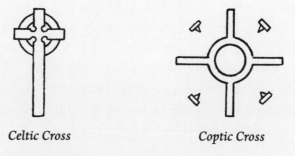

Celtic Cross   Coptic Cross

Crosses and Variations *(continued)*

Cramponnée Cross

Croissantée Cross

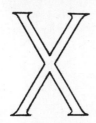

Cross of Lorraine

Crosslet Cross

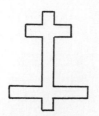

Crux Décussata

Eastern Cross

Fichée Cross

Fitchée Cross

Crosses and Variations *(continued)*

Fretée Cross

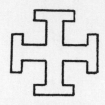

Jerusalem Cross

Maltese Cross

Papal Cross

Monograms of Christ (i)

Monograms of Christ (ii)

Fish (vesica piscis)

The fish, as a Christian symbol, was again taken from Paganism. The son of the sea goddess Atargatis (also known as Aphrodite, Delphine, Derceto, Pelagia, and Tirgata) was Ichthys, which is also the Greek word for "fish." At some point it was suggested that *ichthys* was an acronym for "Jesus Christ, Son of God," and the fish became a Christian symbol. Ichthys was also the name of the fish that swallowed Osiris' penis, and is generally associated with female genital symbolism.

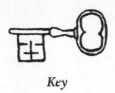

Key

The key is accepted, in Christianity, as representing St. Peter. It is, in effect, the key to the door into the Christian heaven. The idea is based on the Pagan goddess Persephone, who possessed the key to Hades, the afterlife.

Orb

The orb, a symbol of the earth, in Christianity is usually presented surmounted by a cross, symbolizing the Church's domination of the earth.

Tau

Star of Bethlehem

The so-called Star of Bethlehem is no more than the Pagan pentagram, symbolizing the life force.

Eight-Pointed Star of Regeneration

Holy Spirit

Ten Disciples of Jesus

Twelve Tribes of Israel

Freemasonry

Freemasonry is a worldwide initiatory fraternity, which is broken into groups known as lodges. Although Freemasonry is publicly acknowledged, with its lodges and meeting places openly identified, its proceedings are supposedly secret. An oath is taken by initiates, who promise to keep the secrets of Freemasonry.

Freemasonry began in medieval times as an association, or trade union, of craftsmen; of workers in stone. The symbols used in today's rites and rituals are based on items connected with the art of building. The teaching of Freemasonry is done primarily through symbolism. There is only space here to show a small, but representative, fraction of the total number of symbols used.

In the late seventeenth century there was a period known as the Age of Accepted Masonry, when nonworkers were allowed to join the established guilds and their lodges. Prior to that time there had been a tradition of apprenticeship for a would-be mason, though many workers who had not apprenticed would also vie for available jobs. Those who had been apprenticed would recognize one another through certain words and handshakes, so that they could distinguish between themselves and the *cowans*, who might not have been properly schooled. Gradually, however, these cowans, and even nonworkers and gentlemen, got into the lodges and some even started new lodges. By the eighteenth century, there were more nonmasons than true masons in the membership, and Freemasonry had become symbolic, or speculative, as it is today. In Robert Plot's *The Natural History of Staffordshire*, published in 1646, he says that the custom of "admitting Men into the Society of Freemasons" was "spread more or less all over the Nation." He found "persons of the most eminent quality, that did not disdain to be of this Fellowship."

Although Masons were obliged to honor God and the Church, Freemasonry came to be condemned by Pope Clement XII in 1738. Since then the Roman Catholic Church has repeatedly excommunicated any of its members who became Masons, holding that by its beliefs and observances, Freemasonry is a deistic or Pagan religion and that the Masonic oath and the secrecy are unlawful. Yet today the Bible is always present on the Masonic altar, and a belief in god is called for. God is, in fact, regarded as the Grand Architect of the world.

Despite his earlier hostility to Freemasonry, Benjamin Franklin was elected Grand Master of Masons in Pennsylvania in 1734, with the beginnings of Freemasonry in America. By the second half of the twentieth century there were fifty independent Grand Lodges in the United States—one in each state—with a total membership of approximately four million men. In Britain there had been three degrees of advancement within Freemasonry: Entered Apprentice, Fellow Craft, and Master Mason. By the end of the eighteenth century this number had increased, though those three remain the basis of the Masonic system. With different Rites—Scottish, York, Cryptic, Capitular, Templar, etc.—there can be found as many as thirty-three degrees, though the thirty-third one is honorary.

Masonic rituals are held in the Lodge Room, which is furnished especially for the ritual. The officers include the Worshipful Master, Senior and Junior Deacons, Senior and Junior Wardens, Treasurer, and Secretary. Outside the main room, the Tyler guards the entrance door.

Square and Compasses

The best-known symbol of Freemasonry is the Square and Compasses. The Square is a symbol of morality and was originally drawn as a true carpenter's square, with one leg longer than the other. American Masons have got into the habit of drawing it not only with equal-length legs, but with inches marked on it, making it a measuring square rather than a trying square (i.e., a 90° measure for testing, or "trying," the accuracy of the edges of bricks and stones). The Compasses are a symbol of virtue. The Square and Compasses have come to be the symbol or badge of Freemasonry. They are often depicted with a letter *G* in the middle. This *G* is said to stand for "God" or for "Geometry," since God is seen as the Grand Architect.

Lodge; Lodges (used in correspondence)

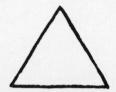

Trinity (a symbol of deity)

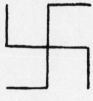

Fylfoot

The Fylfoot, or Jaina Cross, is one of the symbols of the degrees in the Scottish Rite system. Its position, and the color of the ink used, indicates the rank of the person whose signature it follows.

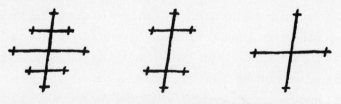

Signature Marks

Here are some examples of Signature Marks, known as *Characteristics*, which were written as prefixes to signatures of

Brethren of the Ancient and Accepted Scottish Rite. Shown are those for the Sovereign Grand Master, Sovereign Grand Inspector General, and Brother, or Sublime Prince, of the Royal Secret. Each is written in red ink.

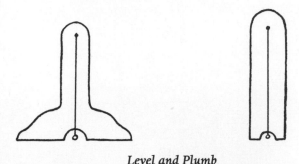

Level and Plumb

The 24" gauge represents the hours of the day and night; the plumb rule, a narrow board with a plum line and plumb bob hanging from it, indicates the true path from which the Mason must not deviate; the gavel symbolizes the power of consciousness; and the chisel represents the advantages of education. The Square, the Level, and the Plumb are called the *Immovable* Jewels of the Lodge, meaning that they have set positions in particular parts of the Lodge: the Square to the east, the Level to the west, and the Plumb to the south.

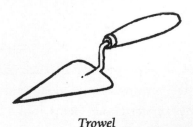

Trowel

The trowel is the working tool of the Master's Degree. It symbolizes the spreading of kindness and affection, to unite the Masonic fraternity.

Gavel

All-Seeing Eye

The All-Seeing Eye is the symbol of the Supreme Omnipresent Deity.

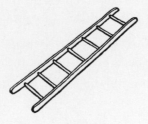

Ladder

The ladder symbolizes progressive advancement. In advanced Freemasonry, there are seven rungs to the ladder, representing Justice, Equity, Kindness, Good Faith, Labor, Patience, and Intelligence. For the First Degree there are only three steps: Faith, Hope, and Charity.

Skull and Cross Bones

The Skull and Cross Bones symbolize mortality and death. In Masonic Templarism, the skull alone is a symbol of mortality. The Skull and Crossbones are used in the Chamber of Reflection, in the French and Scottish Rites, as a trigger to the mind for contemplation of serious subjects.

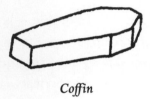

Coffin

The coffin is part of the symbolism of the Third Degree; this is part of the palingenesis, the symbolical death and rebirth motif.

Winding Stairs

The symbol of the Winding Stairs was adopted by the Freemasons of the eighteenth century and introduced into the Fellow

Craft's Degree in the American Rite. In the Ancient and Accepted Scottish Rite, the Winding Stairs are known as *cochleus*, a spiral staircase. The number of steps have varied: five, seven, fifteen, thirty-eight, etc. The Candidate for the degree climbs the stairs, pausing at intervals to receive further knowledge.

Broken Column

Part of the Third-Degree symbolism is known as the *Monument* and shows the scene of a weeping virgin holding a sprig of acacia in one hand and an urn in the other, with a broken column before her. On the column rests a copy of the *Book of Constitutions* (the rules and regulations for the government of the fraternity of Freemasons). Behind her, Time tries to disentangle her hair. Each component of the scene is part of the complex symbolism of Freemasonry.

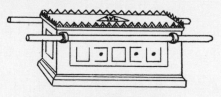

Ark, or Substitute Ark

The Ark, or Substitute Ark, is used in the ceremonies of a Chapter of Royal Arch Masons, and in a Council of Select Masters according to the American system. It is based on the Ark of the Covenant.

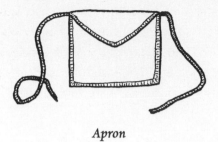

Apron

According to the *Encyclopedia of Freemasonry and Kindred Sciences*, written by Albert G. Mackey and revised and enlarged by Robert I. Clegg, "There is no one of the symbols of Speculative Freemasonry more important in its teachings, or more interesting in its history, than the lambskin, or white leather apron." It is the first gift received by a neophyte. Initially varying in form, according to the whim of the owner, in 1813 the Union of Grand Lodges established a standard for color, material, and size. Other than blue edging and, for some degrees, three rosettes, the apron should be plain. This was in sharp contrast to earlier ones, which were frequently smothered in painted or embroidered symbols.

ᚷNOSTIC

The name *Gnostic* comes from the Greek *gnostikos*, meaning "those who know." It was originally applied to a sect that started in the eastern part of the Roman Empire in the first and second centuries C.E. The Gnostic doctrine was a mixture of Babylonian, Egyptian, Indian, Christian, and Judaic beliefs, with some astrology and magic thrown in. The "knowledge" came from inspiration and revelation, rather than from learning and experiencing.

Gnostic priests would make talismans and charms, and perform exorcisms. The Carpocratians—one of the Gnostic sects—tied in their rites and mysteries with those of the Egyptian goddess Isis. The Simonians (named after Simon Magus, a Jewish heterodox teacher and later a prominent Gnostic) saw much of their mysteries in the symbolism they found in the Book of Genesis (in the Bible). Simon Magus stated that the image of Sophia, the "first idea of God," generated the world. The Ophites also adopted Egyptian rites and had a serpent present as the focus of their rituals.

The basic teachings were believed to come "from the heart," rather than from scientific or even philosophical knowledge. Where other religions were god-centered, the Gnostics were self-centered. Many of the major Gnostic systems were inspired by personal experiences, with a focus on god as a suffering deity. They thought the world was created and ruled by evil powers. They rejected the god of the Jews to the status of demiurge and similarly rejected the Old Testament. Talismans were needed to protect and ward off the ever-present evil.

The Valentinians (a sect named after the most prominent leader of the Gnostic movement, the Roman Valentinus) said that "Gnostics know that they were originally spiritual beings who have come to live in souls and bodies; they once dwelt in the spiritual world above but have been made to fall into this world of sense and sin."[1]

The symbols of Gnosticism were mainly taken from elsewhere and used to assist in the propagation of their beliefs. Many were taken from Semitic and other sources. The numerous astrological symbols seen on many of the Gnostic talismans came from Babylonia and Sumeria.

Chnoubis

Here is Chnoubis over a Bacchic altar, with words meaning "I, even I, am the Good Spirit." Chnoubis is associated with the serpent seen on the staff of Aesculapius (see the chapter on Greek and Roman symbols), and is regarded as a god of healing and a renewer of life.

1. J. J. Hurtak, trans., *Pristis Sophia* (Pretoria: Academy of Future Sciences, 1999).

Abraxas

The god Abraxas, or Anguipede, has the head of a cockerel, a human body, and legs that are serpents. Abraxas is an All-God, or Pantheus.

Ouroboros

Ouroboros, the Gnostic name for the great World Serpent, is a serpent biting its own tail (and also the alchemical symbol for completion; see the chapter on Alchemy). It symbolizes the enclosure of the whole world. To the Gnostics it was also known as Nahash, and Nehushtan. The snake was an important symbol for the Gnostics, especially the Naassene sect, whose name comes from *naas*, "snake."

World Triad

Found in Japan as *mitsu tomoe* and in Tibet as the Cosmic Mandala, the World Triad was adopted by the Gnostics as a symbol for the threefold nature of destiny. It can also be found as symbolizing eternity.

Harpokrates

Here, Harpokrates, the Child Horus, is seated on a lotus and is in the magical boat of IAΩ. One end of the boat terminates in the head of Horus, and the other end terminates in the head of Anubis in the form of an ass. There is a crescent moon and the morning star.

GREEK AND ROMAN

It has been said that it was in Greece that the ancient world rose to its greatest height of creativity. Certainly a wealth of material has been left to us in the myths and legends of those people. Their religious views and their closeness with the deities were both vivid and realistic. The sense of the gods and goddesses was an accepted part of everyday life. Notable was the understanding that, however gifted, the gods were always ready and willing, if not eager, for association with mortals—a trait today found perhaps only in such a chthonic religion as Voudoun.

The Romans were a less imaginative, if more practical, people than the Greeks. Most of their deities were equivalent ones to those the Greeks worshipped, albeit with different (Roman) names.[1] In fact, much of Roman religion came from the Greeks by way of the Etruscans, who were in the northern area of Italy and flourished between 900 and 500 B.C.E. The Roman religious rites were also more formal than those

---

1. The Roman gods are shown in **bold type** in this chapter.

of the Greeks, with more importance given to the days of worship and the actual form of ritual.

The Greeks borrowed many of their magical practices, along with the zodiac, from the Babylonians. However, the majority of symbols found in Greek and Roman religion are the attributes of the various gods and goddesses. Where would Poseidon/**Neptune** be without his trident, or Hermes without the caduceus? There were also carryovers from the Egyptians, such as the Eye of Horus used as a protective symbol.

Prow of Boat Eye

From Phoenician warboats and merchantmen of 750 B.C.E. to the Greek war galleys and merchantmen of 250 B.C.E. and beyond, the protective eye would be painted on the bows of the vessel to look out for danger and to "see" where the ship was going.

Phallus

A belief in the Evil Eye was common in both the Greek and Roman cultures. The idea that some people have the power to cause harm to others—whether intentionally or unconsciously

—simply by looking at them, is an almost universal belief. The Greek word βασκινειν means "to kill with a glance of the eye." The countermeasure for this was a model of a phallus.

Rod of Asclepius/Aesculapius (caduceus)

Asclepius was the son of Apollo and Coronis. He was taught medicine by the centaur Chiron and went on to make many miraculous cures, including bringing the dead back to life. One of his daughters was Hygieia, who became goddess of health. The symbol of Asclepius was a rod around which twined two serpents. This was later inherited by Hermes/**Mercury** as the caduceus. In fact, the serpent-entwined rod came originally from the Sumerian god Ningishzida, the son of the Mater-physician Ninazu.

Cornucopia

Copia was the Roman goddess of plenty, sometimes identified with the Greek goddess Tyche. *Cornucopia* means "horn of Copia," i.e., "horn of plenty." It was a magic horn that provided everything its owner desired. Other deities, in addition to Copia, are depicted holding the cornucopia (e.g., Banda, Cernunnos, Eirene, **Fortuna**, **Pax**, Rosmerta, Tutela, **Virtus**).

Thunderbolt—Zeus/Jupiter

The head of the Greek's Olympian pantheon was Zeus, father and king of gods and men. His Roman counterpart was **Jupiter**. Poseidon/**Neptune** and Hades/**Pluto** were his brothers. Zeus became omnipotent and omniscient, the fountainhead of divination. One of his attributes is the eagle. Another is the thunderbolt, which he was capable of flinging at those who displeased him. He was lord of the winds, clouds, rain, and thunder.

Trident

Poseidon was the brother of Zeus and ruled the seas and the oceans. He could split rocks with his trident, thus acquiring the epithet "earth shaker." He was equated with the Roman god **Neptune**. It is said that the three prongs of the trident represent the past, present, and future. The trident is also found with the Hindu god Shiva, where the three prongs represent his function as creator, destroyer, and preserver. (See also the chapter on Hindu symbols.)

Owl

Athena/**Minerva** was goddess of both war and wisdom. She was the daughter of Zeus and Metis. Her patron bird was the owl, also the totem bird of Athens. On the breastplate of her armor she wears the aegis and the head of Medusa, the Gorgon.

Medusa's Head (Gorgon)

Hammer & Tongs of Hephaestus/Vulcan

Hephaestus was the Greek god of metalwork and craftsman-ship. He is equated with the Roman god **Vulcan**. He was born lame, for which his mother, Hera, threw him down from Olympus. But he went on to become a skilled workman and a great smith of the gods.

The Corn Sheaf

Torch

The Corn Sheaf was the symbol of the Great Mysteries at Eleusis, and of all corn deities. Wheat and corn sheaves sym-

bolize the fertility of the earth. It is the symbol of Demeter/
Ceres. The Eleusinian Mysteries were founded on the myth
of Demeter's journey through the underworld in search of
her daughter Persephone (also known as Kore), who had been
abducted by Hades. The Mysteries was a major festival cele-
brating first (in October) the disappearance of Persephone,
and then (in February) her return. Along with the sheaf,
Demeter's other attribute is the torch, symbolizing her search
in the netherworld.

Labrys

Much as Demeter roamed the underworld in her search for
Persephone, so did Theseus have to travel through the labyrinth
of Knossos, in Crete, in search of the Minotaur. With the aid
of Ariadne, he found and killed the Minotaur. The symbol of
Knossos was the Labrys, the double-bladed axe, which has, in
recent times, become a symbol of lesbianism because of its
association with the Amazons.

Labyrinth

Thyrsus

The Thyrsus was the sacred rod of Dionysus/**Bacchus**. It was
a stalk of fennel topped by a pine cone and represented the
phallus, a fertility symbol. The Roman name for the thyrsus
was *baculus*, after the god **Bacchus**.

ℌINDU

Om, or *AUM,* is believed to be the one eternal symbol incorporating past, present, and future. Some say the three letters of AUM stand for Brahma, Vishnu, and Shiva; Creator, Preserver, and Destroyer. The word is a shortened version of the whole phrase *Aum-mani-padme-hum.* According to *The Theosophical Glossary* of Helena P. Blavatsky:

"Om! the jewel in the lotus, hum! One of the most sacred Buddhist mantras or verbal formulas; used very frequently in Tibet and in surrounding countries of the Far East. Not only is every syllable said to have a secret power of producing a definite result, but the whole invocation has a number of meanings. When properly pronounced or changed, it produces different results, differing from the others according to the intonation and will given to the formula and its syllables. This mystic sentence above all refers to the indissoluble union between man and the universe, and thus conveys 'I am in thee and thou art in me.' Each of us has within himself the jewel in the lotus or the divine self within. When understood in a kosmic sense, it signifies the divine kosmic self within, inspiring all beings within the range of that kosmic divinity."[1]

Two versions of the symbol for Om

Tattvas

One of the systems for classifying the five elements—water, air, fire, earth, spirit—in Hinduism is with the use of *tattvas*. Water is represented by a silver crescent moon, Air is a blue circle, Fire is a red triangle, Earth is a yellow diamond, and Spirit is an indigo egg. The names of the tattvas are the names of deities: Apas, Vayu, Tejas, Prithivi, and Akasa. The appropriate tattva may be used in ritual to summon one of the deities.

---

1. Helena P. Blavatsky, *The Theosophical Glossary* (London: Theosophical Publishing Society, 1892).

ISLAM

Islam is Arabic for "submission" (to the will of God). It is the name given by Moslems to their religion. Approximately one-fifth of the world's population is Muslim. Muhammad is regarded as the last of the great prophets. To him God gave a book, the *Qur'an*, or Koran (as God gave the Torah to Moses), and revealed himself to humankind through that book. Muslims believe that their religion was the one revealed to all the prophets. Islam is a way of life, with every aspect exhaustively examined, with thorough guidelines. There is also a belief in an afterlife, as detailed as the present life. This afterlife is written about in both the Qur'an and the *Hadith* (the sayings of Muhammad).

When he was forty years old, Muhammad spent a night in a cave, where he was visited by the Angel Gabriel, or *Jibril*. There he received the first of the communications from Allah. These contacts continued for twenty-three years. The words he received, Muhammad recited at Ramadan (the ninth month of the Muslim calendar), in the year 610 C.E. Every year thereafter, at that time, he would recite all that he had received. It has been said that Islam owes everything to Muhammad, because of his profound religious insight, his organizational talent, and his political leadership.

The early forging of Islam in effect attacked the polytheism that predated it, bringing in a form of monotheism. However, as with Christianity's inability to completely erase Paganism, so Islam was unable to completely eradicate the worship of stones, trees, and nature. Today, relics and fetishes are in constant demand, and ancient places of worship are now ascribed to saints and prophets.

Star & Crescent

Adopted as the symbol of Islam in the fourteenth century, this waxing moon (associated with Diana) was used first and then the star was added later, as a symbol of divinity and sovereignty. In ancient Asia, the crescent moon represented the barque of Sin, the Babylonian moon-god.

Hand of Fatima

Named after Muhammad's daughter, the Hand of Fatima represents the Five Pillars of Islam; the five fundamentals: faith, prayer, pilgrimage, fasting, and charity. Also, the thumb represents the Prophet, the first finger is the Lady Fatima, the second finger is her husband, Ali, and the third and fourth fingers are their sons Hasan and Husain.

JUDAIC

Judaism is one of the three great theocentric faiths (the other two being Christianity and Islam, both stemming from Judaism); faiths centered around a personal god and propagated by prophets. Prior to the founding of Judaism there was another attempt to found a monotheistic religion and that was in 1380 B.C.E., when Amenhotep IV promoted a solar deity in Egypt. The god of the Jews was originally *Jahweh*, possibly a Sinaitic thunder god from the south of Mesopotamia. He was promoted by Moses and assimilated with *El-Shaddai*, god of the mountains of Northern Mesopotamia. A succession of prophets, including Abraham, Elijah, Moses, and Jeremiah, developed the worship of this god to the point where they drove out the natural polytheism of their people. Previously nature worshippers, with emphasis on agriculture and fertility, the communities included Astarte in their original worship and incorporated the veneration of trees, streams, wells, stones, and serpents.

After a very stormy history, by the early Middle Ages the Jews had compiled the *Talmud*. This was a collection of all the various sources of written and unwritten law, put together with both traditional interpretations and the opinions of generations of rabbis. It embodied legends and sermons, and was finally completed by the end of the fifth century. It comprised sixty-three volumes. The first five books of this Hebrew Bible comprise the *Torah*.

By the thirteenth century another movement had arisen. This was mystical in nature, and its various books of speculative theology and mystical number symbolism was called the *Kabbalah*. The Torah has four levels of meaning: the literal, the allegorical, the homiletical (sermons, moral lectures), and the mystical. The Kabbalah is part of the mysticism of the Torah. It states that there is a series of ten spheres, or *sefirot*, through which divine influence passes to reach the earth. The central text is known as the *Zohar*, which shows the tenth sefirah as being a feminine aspect of deity. This is called *Shekhinah*. The Zohar is believed to be the teachings of the third-century Rabbi Simeon bar Yochai.

The Star of David

The Star of David is the magical hexagram. It was early revered in India as a symbol of the union between Shiva and Kali and is found in the Hindu emblem Sri Iantra. It was only officially accepted as a Jewish symbol in relatively modern times, in 1897.

The Menorah

The Menorah is the seven-branched candleholder. The seven branches represent the seven days of the week. It is said that they also represent the sun, the moon, and the five main planets. The three U-shaped arms are for beauty, strength, and wisdom.

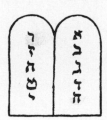 

The Commandment Tablets   *The Pentateuch (the Torah)*

Adonai

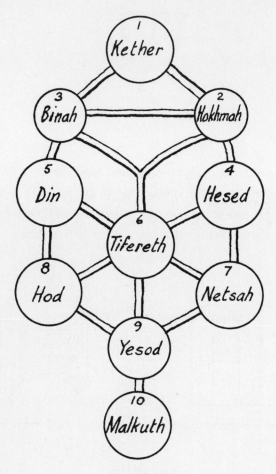

Tree of Life

Here is the Tree of Life, showing the ten spheres (sefirot).

1: Kether—Supreme Crown

2: Hokhmah—Wisdom

3: Binah—Understanding

4: Hesed—Love

5: Din—Power

6: Tifereth—Beauty

7: Netsah—Endurance

8: Hod—Majesty

9: Yesod—Foundation

10: Malkuth—Kingdom

Magical Alphabets

In the Middle Ages, Ceremonial Magic was openly practiced by many high dignitaries of the Christian Church. (See also the chapter on Ceremonial Magic.) This was a time when the Church was mercilessly persecuting people for being Witches. However, since Ceremonial Magic was regarded as a practice rather than a religion, it was not viewed as being counter to the Church teachings and a blind eye was turned to those who performed it.

There was great rivalry between the magicians, who usually worked alone and jealously guarded the methods of operation they perfected. To safeguard the results of countless years of work, many magicians would write the most important parts of their *grimoires*, or books of magic, in secret, "magical" alphabets. This way, if the book was ever stolen, the thief would not necessarily be able to perform the work it had taken so many years for the magician to perfect.

Various magical alphabets were used to preserve this secrecy. They had such titles as *Angelic, Enochian, Malachim* (or

Language of the Magi), Ogham, *Passing the River*, and *Theban*. Various of the runic alphabets were also employed, as were Egyptian hieroglyphics.

But perhaps the more important reason for using the magical alphabets was power: power that the magician could put into his book and into the talismans and other instruments he used. Everything used had to be powerful enough to protect the magician from the wrath of the entities he summoned. If using ordinary, everyday writing, overfamiliarity would bring about a tendency to scribble down what was to be recorded without really thinking about the actual writing itself; the formation of the individual letters. But if using an alphabet with which he was not too familiar, the magician would really have to concentrate on the actual forming of every letter. In this way, according to the old grimoires, he would be putting his energies, his "power" or *mana*, into that writing.

This was especially important in the writing used on such things as talismans, for the more power that went into the making of a talisman, the better; the more protective it would be. Magical alphabets were therefore used both for secrecy and for directing energy into what was being written.

Some of these magical alphabets are still used by modern-day magicians and Witches. However, many who use them have forgotten, or are ignorant of, the original reasons for their use. They will try to impress others by showing their proficiency with, for example, Theban, writing it as rapidly as they would everyday English. Doing this, however, actually shows tremendous ignorance, since it defeats the whole purpose of using the magical writing.

In the making of talismans, magicians will often utilize what are known as *magic squares*. A magic square is an arrangement of numbers, in the form of a square, where every row and column, plus both diagonals, add up to the same number, called the *constant*. Each number may only appear once in the square. These magic squares were originally used in ancient India and China, and were introduced into Europe early in the Christian era. Sometimes letters are used instead of numbers, and then one of the magical alphabets is utilized.

Cornelius Agrippa (1486–1535), whose real name was Heinrich Cornelis, constructed seven different magic squares that he aligned with the seven planets: Saturn, Jupiter, Mars, the Sun, Venus, Mercury, and the Moon. These have become standards in ritual magic. The Saturn square is probably one of the oldest, being found in the Chinese I Ching. Its constant is 15. Agrippa founded several secret magical societies and wrote a number of books on magic.

Francis Barrett, in his *The Magus* (1801), Eliphas Levi, in *Transcendental Magic* (1896), and others, followed the lead of Agrippa, employing magic squares for a variety of purposes, from protection in childbirth to making a man powerful. In S. L. MacGregor Mathers's translation of *The Book of Sacred Magic of Abra-Melin the Mage*, published in 1932, the book shows a large number of magic squares for many different purposes, the majority comprised of letters rather than numbers. These are arranged so that the words read the same from the left, right, downward, and upward. One of these, known as the *Sator formula*—from the first word across the top of the square—was discovered engraved on old drinking vessels and on fragments from a Roman villa near Cirencester, England (see illustration at the end of this chapter).

Great care is necessary when constructing magic squares. Usually drawn on parchment, the lines should be marked in black ink with the numbers or letters in red ink. The red should not touch the black anywhere. All should be drawn with the parchment set up so that the maker's shadow does not fall on the work.

Magical Alphabets

𐤗 ᛉ ᚾ ᚦ ᛏ ᚦ ᚦ ᛏ ᚦ ᛒ ᚷ ᛕ

A B C D E F G H I,J K L M

ᛋ ᛃ ᛩ ᛄ ᚢ ᚢ ᛁ ᛲ ᛋ ᛟ

N O,Q P R S T U,V W X Y Z

Angelic, or Celestial

This magical alphabet was so-called because it was thought to tie in with the placing of the stars.

𐌗 ᚢ ᛒ ᛝ ᛏ ᛝ ᛭ ᛚ ᛗ ᛚ ᛖ Ɛ

A B C,K D E F G H,I,Y,J L M

Ᵹ ᛚ ᚲ ᚢ Ɛᛃ ᚾ ᛚ ᚧ ᚦ

N O P Q R S T U,V,W X Z

Enochian

The Enochian magical alphabet comes from the system of magic introduced by Dr. John Dee (Astrologer Royal to Queen Elizabeth I) in the sixteenth century. It became a part of the Hermetic Order of the Golden Dawn and was used by such magicians as Aleister Crowley. Enochian is interesting in that the alphabet appears unrelated to any previous lettering system and the language has its own unique grammar.

Magical Alphabets *(continued)*

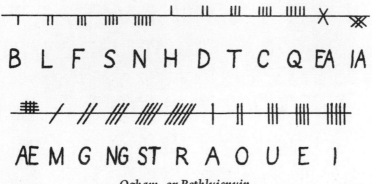

Malachim, or Language/Writing of the Magi

Ogham, or Bethluisnuin

Ogham (pronounced *OH-yam*), or Ogam (*Ohm*), was originally used by the early Celts and their priests, the Druids, and was probably developed between the second and third centuries c.e., though some Celtic scholars believe it to be far older. It was used mainly on boundary markers and on grave stones, carved into the stone or wood along an edge, hence the center line. It was read from top to bottom and left to right. There are 369 verified examples of Ogham writing surviving today.

Magical Alphabets *(continued)*

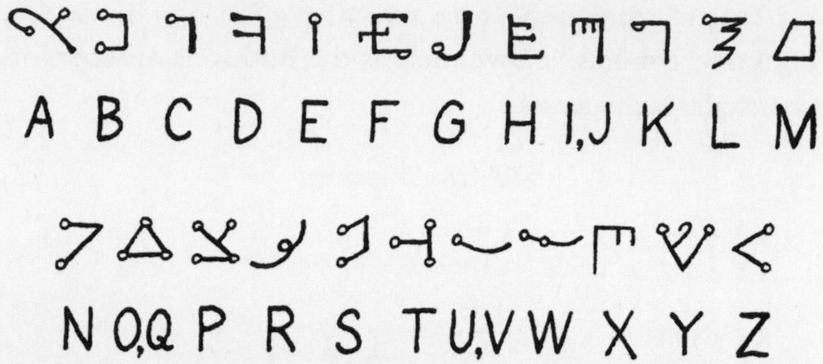

A B C D E F G H I,J K L M

N O,Q P R S T U,V W X Y Z

Passing the River

A B C D E F G H I,J K L M N

O P Q R S T U,V W X Y Z END

Theban, or Honorian

F U TH O R C G W H N I J ė P

X,Z S T B E NG D L M OE A AE Y EA

Runes, Anglo-Saxon—Ruthwell

There are many variations on the runes, the three main types being Germanic, Scandinavian, and Anglo-Saxon.

Each of these, in turn, has variations. (See also the chapter on Runic symbols.) Shown here is the Ruthwell variation of the Anglo-Saxon runes.

Magic Squares

4	9	2
3	5	7
8	1	6

Square of Saturn

4	14	15	1
9	7	6	12
5	11	10	8
16	2	3	13

Square of Jupiter

11	24	7	20	3
4	12	25	8	16
17	5	13	21	9
10	18	1	14	22
23	6	19	2	15

Square of Mars

Magic Squares *(continued)*

6	32	3	34	35	1
7	11	27	28	8	30
19	14	16	15	23	24
18	20	22	21	17	13
25	29	10	9	26	12
36	5	33	4	2	31

Square of the Sun

22	47	16	41	10	35	4
5	23	43	17	42	11	29
30	6	24	49	81	36	12
13	31	7	25	43	19	37
38	14	32	1	26	44	20
21	39	8	33	2	27	45
46	15	40	9	34	3	28

Square of Venus

Magic Squares *(continued)*

8	58	59	5	4	62	63	1
49	15	14	52	53	11	10	56
41	23	22	44	48	19	18	45
32	34	38	29	25	35	39	28
40	26	27	37	36	30	31	33
17	47	46	20	21	43	42	24
9	55	54	12	13	51	50	16
64	2	3	61	60	6	7	57

Square of Mercury

37	78	29	70	21	62	13	54	5
6	38	79	30	71	22	63	14	46
47	7	39	80	31	72	23	55	15
16	48	8	40	81	32	64	24	56
57	17	49	9	41	73	33	65	25
26	58	18	50	1	42	74	34	66
67	27	59	10	51	2	43	75	35
36	68	19	60	11	52	3	44	76
77	28	69	20	61	12	53	4	45

Square of the Moon

Sator Square

Typical of magical squares using letters rather than numbers is the so-called Sator square, shown here with letters and also with those letters written using the Theban alphabet. It has been suggested that the Sator square is based on the letters of the Christian *Pater noster* (The Lord's Prayer), but there is no real evidence of that. Also shown is the Milon square (done in letters and in runes), which allows its maker to "know all things past and future," according to *The Book of Sacred Magic of Abra-Melin the Mage*. It is possibly derived from the Hebrew MLVN, which is "a diversity of things or matters."

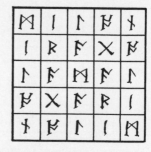

Sator Square

Milon Square

Native American

According to the U.S. Department of the Interior Bureau of Indian Affairs, among Native Americans the word *tribe* originally meant a body of persons bound together by blood ties who were socially, politically, and religiously organized and who lived together, occupying a definite territory, and spoke a common language or dialect. But with the organizing of reservations, the word *tribe* developed a number of different meanings. Today it can be a distinct group within a village or community, the entire community, a large number of communities, several different groups or villages speaking different languages but sharing a common government, or a widely scattered number of villages with a common language but no common government. The Bureau of Indian Affairs counts 263 tribes, bands, villages, pueblos, and groups in states other than Alaska, and approximately 300 Native Alaskan communities.

In the east, from the Great Lakes south to the Gulf of Mexico, there were the *woodsmen of the eastern forests*, who traveled by foot or canoe, living mostly by hunting, fishing, and berry-picking. In the central United States were the *hunters of the plain*. They lived west of the Mississippi and east of the Rockies, extending from Montana and the Dakotas south to Texas. Acquiring horses from the Spaniards, they hunted buffalo over great areas of the West. In the rest of the country were several smaller groups such as the *northern fishermen* of the forest and river valleys of Washington and Oregon; the *seed gatherers* of California, Nevada, and Utah; the *Navaho shepherds* of Arizona; the *Pueblo farmers* of New Mexico; and the *desert dwellers* of southern Arizona and New Mexico. In Alaska are the *woodsmen of the North* and the Point Barrow, Bering Strait, and Pacific Eskimo.

There are eight major linguistic groups: the Algonquian, Iroquian, Cadoean, Muskhogean, Siouan, Penutian, Athapascan, and the Uto-Aztecan.

Native American religions were expressed in dances, ceremonials, and through storytelling of myths and legends. Except among the Southwest pueblos, visions and dreams were sought as sources of power. Prayers were addressed to natural factors such as the sun, the winds, thunder, and the earth. These were all symbols of supernatural power, and deities appeared and were shown in sculpture and paintings.

Pictures were painted on the sides of tepees, on drums, and on clothing such as shirts, breech clouts, armbands, legging strips, vests, and the like. Designs were incorporated into pottery, baskets, and beadwork. Many design figures were common to several tribes while other figures were peculiar to a specific area. The Blackfoot, for example, mainly used geometric shapes, while the Crow used a lot of floral designs.

Although there was no written language before contact with non-natives, in the sense of symbols for letters and full alphabets, there were early records in the form of pictographs. Some of these showed objects such as birds, animals, mountains, and the sun, while others showed abstract concepts such as death, famine, ancestors, and directions.

Across North America there was belief in many different deities. There were also many different beliefs about life, death, the afterlife, and the origins of humankind. All Native Americans, however, held to the tenet that every living thing—humans, animals, *and* plants—had a soul and should be respected.

Mother Earth (Hopi)

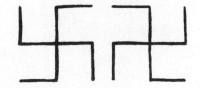

Swastika (Hopi)   (i) Earth   (ii) Sun

Horned Serpent

Butterfly (Hopi)

Sacred Fire (Desena)

Esoteric Aspects of the Sacred Fire (Anasazi)

Medicine Shield—the Universe (Sioux)

Medicine Path (Pueblo)

Sweat Lodge (Sioux)

Thunderbird—Rain Bridge (Dakota)

Bear Clan (Hopi)

Horse

Coyote

Spider (Osage and Omaha)

Deer

Head of Brown Bear (Chilkat)

Bear's Paws and Forelegs (Chilkat)

Man

Woman

Friendship

Clouds

Frog Head (Chilkat)

Turtle

Kókopilau, the Hunchback Flute
Player (Hopi)

Wa-Hun-De-Dan
—Goddess of War

Mana-Bozho—God of Fire,
Dawn, and Air

Manito, the Great Spirit

Athenesic—Moon Goddess

Unkatah—
Goddess Against Disease

Taknokwumu—Spirit Who
Rules Weather (Hopi Fire Clan)

Bad Spirit of the Dark Sky

Good Spirit of the Blue Sky

Pálulukang—Feathered (Water) Snake (Hopi)

Yo-He-Wah—Spirit of the Grass

Haokah the Giant (Sioux)

Animiki—God of Storm and Thunder

Spirit of Evil

Life-Giving Rain

Path of Learning

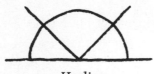

Healing

Sky Coyote

Sandpaintings are done by the Navajo. While most other tribes would treat sickness with herbal cures, the Navajo believe that most illnesses are caused by evil spirits and bewitchment. They therefore attempt to exorcise the afflicted person in elaborate ceremonies utilizing dry "paintings." These are constructed of ground minerals, such as sandstone, charcoal, gypsum, and ocher, placed on a bed of sand. Bright colors of black, white, red, yellow, and blue are produced. Some of the designs are so intricate that it can take up to fifteen men a full day to complete the painting. There are literally hundreds of different designs, depending upon what is thought to be the cause of the malady. The ritual of making the painting is led by a shaman. When the painting is finished, the afflicted person will stand, kneel, or lie on it so that its power may penetrate. The shaman, meanwhile, will pray, chant, and shake his rattle to bring about the cure. The painting is destroyed immediately after use, though everyone in the hogan where the ritual took place may take a small pinch of the magical powder.

*Healing Painting—The four female figures represent the four
elements and the four cardinal points.*

Archeological evidence indicates that a new religious cult
began to flourish in a number of Mississippian centers around
1200 C.E. Known as the Buzzard, or Southern, Cult, its origins
are not known, yet many of its symbols are similar to those of
Mesoamerica. There are many variations on the main figures,
which are shown here:

Cross

Sun Circle

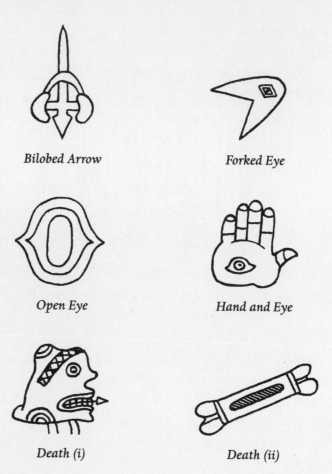

Bilobed Arrow

Forked Eye

Open Eye

Hand and Eye

Death (i)

Death (ii)

Kachinas are benevolent spirits who live among the Hopi for six months out of every year. The first ones begin to arrive in December. Many more then arrive in February, during the Powamuya season. At this time there is a ceremony with the Hopi ritually acting out the final stages of the creation of the world. In this, they call upon the kachina spirits to bring growth and maturity to all humankind. Some months later, after the July Niman ceremony, the kachinas return to their spirit world. Kachina dolls, therefore, are not just carved figurines; they have important meaning to the Hopi people who believe they are personifications of the kachina spirits.

There are several hundred kachinas. Here are just a few representative ones.

Medicine Man

The Medicine Man possesses the power to cure and to prevent sickness and disease.

Badger

Known for his wisdom, Badger has a great knowledge of herbs and is able to cure the sick.

Deer

Deer brings plenty of game to be hunted.

Fox Warrior

Fox Warrior represents the spirit of the fox and is a runner.

Kachina Masks

Three-Horned

Broad-Faced

Black Mask

Snow

Kachina Masks *(continued)*

Saviki

Tasaf Anya

Hano Clown

Sun

ᛚORSE

The Eddas and Sagas—the anonymously written collections of the oral histories—preserve the songs of the Northern scalds, or poets, telling of the creation myths. They tell of how, in the beginning when there was nothing, whatever the Allfather willed came to pass. Various creatures came into being, including the giants, who became enemies of the gods. First came Surtr, then Ymir (or Orgelmir), then Buri and Thrudgelmir, and others. When Börr, son of the god Buri, married Bestla, they produced three sons. One of these sons was named Odin, which means "spirit."

In Northern mythology, the gods are called the *Æsir* ("supporters" or "pillars of the world"). They built the world on the dead body of the giant Ymir, whom they finally slew. The center of his body was named Midgard, which means "middle garden." This was for humans. To support the heavens, four strong dwarves were employed: Nordri, in the north; Sudri, in the south; Austri, in the east; and Vestri, in the west. An area called Asgard was set aside for the gods. This was where the twelve gods and twenty-four goddesses lived, led by Odin.

Odin (also called Wuotan, or Woden) was the highest, holiest of the gods. He was given the surname Allfather. Two ravens, Hugin ("thought") and Munin ("memory") perched on his shoulders. They would fly out each day and return to report all that was taking place. At Odin's feet lay two wolf-hounds, Geri and Freki.

Allfather created a huge ash tree called Yggdrasil: the tree of the universe, of time, and of life. Its roots reached down to the remotest depths of Niflheim (the realm of the dead) and the spring Hvergelmir, and its evergreen branches (the top one named Lerad) reached up to overshadow Odin's hall. Various creatures lived in and on the tree.

Odin was the inventor of the runes, the earliest form of writing used in Northern lands. (See also the chapter on Runic symbols.) The characters were first used only for divination but later for the writing of records, inscriptions, and other things. It was believed that wisdom only came through sacrifice, so Odin hung for nine days and nights from the sacred tree Yggdrasil to obtain the knowledge of the runes. He wounded himself with his spear, Gungnir, and hung, gazing down into the immeasurable depths of Niflheim, before gaining that knowledge. This then gave him power over all things. He cut a runic inscription into his spear, and even engraved runes on the teeth of his horse, Sleipnir.

Sleipnir, Odin's Horse

Odin rode Sleipnir in the Wild Hunt (the sound of rushing wind came to be associated with the sound of Odin hunting). Since Odin was among other things a wind god, his horse had eight feet, for speed.

Thor's Hammer

Thor's Hammer is often carried as a talisman. It protects against fire, thunder, and lightning, and serves as a general protection. In the North, Thor's Hammer has rivaled the crucifix as a sacred symbol.

Wotan's Cross

Wotan's Cross is sometimes called the Sun Cross.

ROSICRUCIAN

The Rosicrucian brotherhood, or society, probably began in the sixteenth century. It has been suggested that the name comes from Christian Rozenkreuze, the founder of the group, but in fact there was no such person. The name more likely is derived from the Latin *rosa*, a rose, and *cruz*, a cross. Very few facts were known about the Rosicrucians until Arthur Edward Waite published his book *The Real History of the Rosicrucians* in 1887. Prior to that, all writings were composed of speculation and pretension. Waite showed that the name Rosicrucian was unknown before 1598. In the opening years of the seventeenth century, a pamphlet was published bearing the title *Fama Fraternitatis*, or *The Fama of the Fraternity of the Meritorious Order of the Rosy Cross Addressed to the Learned in General and the Governors of Europe*. The pamphlet was supposedly authored by a number of anonymous mystics who were concerned about the state of humanity and encouraged the coming together of the learned of the world, assisted by themselves—authorities who had been initiated into the mysteries. They detailed a long and involved history of the founder of their fraternity, who had traveled extensively and learned the many great secrets of the adepts. Now, three generations later, they said, the descendants of the order were looking to initiate others. The authors of this pamphlet created much curiosity and excitement throughout Europe, where many occultists applied to join. However, no response came to these applications and eventually it was felt that the whole story had been a hoax.

But the idea of an ancient secret society of occult adepts had hit a nerve. *The Chymical Nuptials of Christian Rosencreutz* was published in 1616, purporting to be the life story of the founder of the mysterious order. However, interest waned and nothing more was heard of the order for at least a century. In 1710, in Germany, a "Sincerus Racatus," or Sigmund Richter, published rules for a Rosicrucian Society and began to initiate members. In 1785 a book was published titled *The Secret Symbols of the Rosicrucians of the Sixteenth and Seventeenth Centuries*. Since then, various individuals have claimed to have been initiated, usually by "a mysterious Rosicrucian" without a name and usually in Germany or close by. The individuals have then gone on to found their own form of the brotherhood.

The Rosicrucian Fellowship was founded by Carl Louis van Grashof (otherwise known as Max Heindel) in 1907. Grashof claimed that on a visit to Europe that year he had been initiated at a Rose Cross temple on the borders of Germany and Bohemia. In 1904 Grashof had been vice president of the Los Angeles lodge of the Theosophical Society, and had come to America from Germany nine years before that.

The Rose Cross Order was founded in 1958, developed from lectures given by Pascal Beverley Randolph, a spiritualist medium and self-styled Professor of Oriental Interior Science. There is also the Rosicrucian Society of England, the *Societas Rosicruciana* in Boston, the *Fraternitas Rosae Crucis* in Pennsylvania, the New Fellowship of the Rosy Cross, and many others. Today there are societies, fellowships, lodges, brotherhoods, and orders throughout the world. Some are secretive and hidden while others are open and active. Most are critical of each other, many claiming to be the only "true" Rosicrucianism.

Perhaps the best known—or most successful, commercially—is *The Ancient and Mystic Order Rosae Crucis (AMORC)*, founded by H. Spencer Lewis in 1915. The majority of Rosicrucian organizations do not proselytize, but AMORC is a mainly commercial organization, advertising extensively in newspapers and magazines and offering correspondence courses. In 1915 Lewis placed an ad in a New York newspaper and so started the AMORC. As with so many others, he claimed to have received special knowledge and authorization to start his order from "Rosicrucian Masters." He made himself the "Supreme Autocratic Authority, Imperator for North, Central, and South America, the British Commonwealth and Empire, France, Switzerland, Sweden and Africa." On Lewis's death in 1939, his son Ralph succeeded him.

There are degrees of advancement in AMORC: three basic degrees, which can be followed by nine "Temple" degrees. These last take the person to the exclusive Illuminati of the order. As with Freemasonry, Rosicrucianism is anathema to the Roman Catholic Church.

Great Seal of the American Supreme Council of AMORC

Official AMORC Rosicrucian Cross

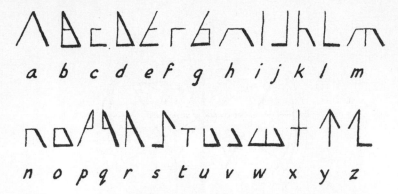

The AMORC Alphabet

The following are some of the many symbols adopted by AMORC:

Pentagram of Faust

Four Kabalistic Names

Hermetic Rose Cross

The Hermetic Rose Cross, according to H. Spencer Lewis, symbolizes "all the majesty, power, beauty, and protection of the Rosicrucian Order."

Great Seal of the Grand Master   *Seal of the Supreme Secretary*

 RUNIC

Rune, meaning "mystery" or "secret," is the name given to an alphabet character found in all Germanic countries. It has been suggested that the runes derive from Greek, but recent evidence seems to support derivation from an Italic alphabet of Etruscan origin. Runes were found in third-century Scandinavia and in remote districts of Sweden down through modern times.

The earliest form of runes had 24 letters and was known as *futhark*, after the first six letters ("th" had a single rune). These 24 were divided into three groups of eight runes, each group known as an *aett* or *aettir* (Scandinavian meaning "number of eight"). The three groups were named after three Norse gods: Freyr, Hagal, and Tyr. Every individual rune had a name and these names were known and recorded in ancient Anglo-Saxon manuscripts.

Mythology tells that the great Norse god Odin hung from the Tree of the World, *Yggdrasil*, for nine days and nights, pierced by a spear. He hung there as a self-sacrifice. At the end of that time, just before he fell, he was able to reach out and grasp the runes, bringing humankind the gift of learning.

Ralph H. Blum, in *The Healing Runes*, says that "from its very inception, runic writing was not primarily utilitarian, and that the evidence of its sacred function is found first in the bonding of secular letters with the pre-runic symbols employed in pagan Germanic rites and religious practices and, even more dramatically, in their association with the Germanic gods, thereby situating the runic alphabet at the very heart of the old German religion."[1] As he points out, to the Pagan everything in nature was alive. Hence, stones and wood were carved to serve as runes for casting, since they embodied the sacred.

Over the centuries runes have been used to foresee the future and to protect, heal, curse, and invoke the gods. They have been used in medicine, magic, and war. They have also been used simply as writing, albeit as magical inscriptions. (See also the chapter on Magical Alphabets.)

Although used for a relatively brief period on the western Germanic continent, the runes were used for many centuries in Britain. New letters were added, giving a total of 28. This increased again in the ninth century, in Northumbria, to 33 runes. The opposite took place in Scandinavia, with the number of runes dropping from 24 to 16. This was due to the same rune being used for a number of different sounds. There were also variations on the runes; the Swedish-Norwegian, for example, differing slightly from the Danish. There is also the Hälsinge version of the runes, named for the region of Hälsingland where they were first found. They seem to be a sort of runic shorthand. By the eleventh century, Norway was using a mixture of Swedish-Norwegian and Danish runes. The Danish, meanwhile, had followed the lead of the Anglo-Saxons and placed an *i* inside a *u* to make a *y*. Out of the *i* they made a special letter for *e*, and out of the *k* a special letter for *g*.

1. Ralph H. Blum, *The Healing Runes* (New York: St. Martin's Press, 1995).

Germanic Runes

ᚠᚢᚦᚨᚱ᚜ᚷᚹ

f u th a r k g w

ᚺᚾᛁᛃᛖᛈ ᚱᛊ

h n i j ė p R s

ᛒᛖᛗᛚᛜᛟᛞ

b e m l ng o d

Germanic

Scandinavian Runes

f u th ą r k h n i a
s t b m l R

Danish

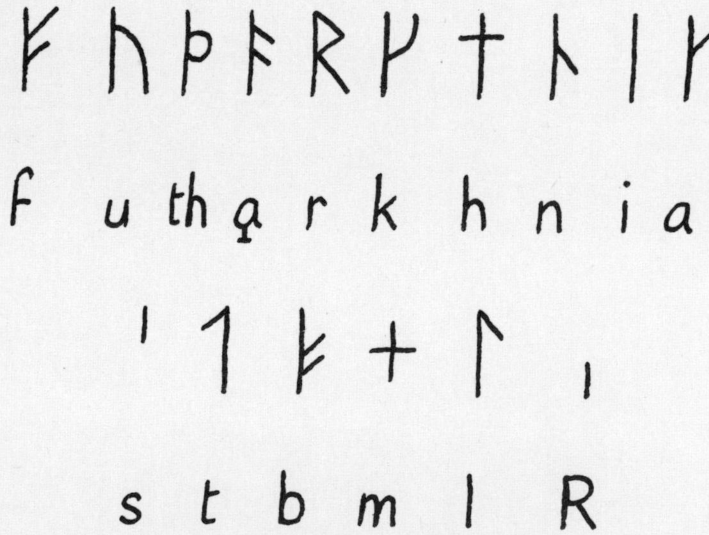
f u th ą r k h n i a
s t b m l R

Swedish-Norwegian

Anglo-Saxon Runes

f   u   th   o   r   c   g   w   h   n

i   j   é   p   z   s   t   b   e

m   l   ng   o   d   a   ae   y   ea

Ruthwell

Anglo-Saxon Runes *(continued)*

Vienna

Anglo-Saxon Runes *(continued)*

Thames

SHINTO

Shinto is a relative newcomer to Japan, with many of its practices and ideas imported from China and Korea. Before the end of the nineteenth century, the honoring of ancestors in Japan was done at Buddhist temples. It was the ending of the Shoguns—supreme military commanders commissioned by early Japanese emperors, who later developed into de facto rulers or administrators of the country—that brought about the introduction of a National or State Shinto. Today, almost every town and village in Japan has Shinto shrines along with Buddhist temples.

The Shinto shrines are frequently located in beautiful, natural surroundings, with an approach path and with the distinctive *torii*, the entrance gateways. Spirit entities are known as *kami*. The shrines are residences for the kami. They are not places for the gathering of people to worship; they are simply the home of the kami. Anyone may enter a shrine. Before they may enter, visitors must rinse out their mouths and rinse their hands with water from a special trough of running water. Only the priests may enter the inner hall, where the kami dwell. To ask the gods for favor, supplicants write their desires on wooden prayer tablets and hang them in the shrine.

Buddhism, Taoism, and Confucianism have all contributed to Shinto. Festivals are popular and elaborate, with processions, contests, dances, and entertainment of all sorts. Many of the festivals contain vestiges of earlier agricultural celebrations. There are several thousand festivals, known as *matsuri*.

In Shinto mythology, two divinities (Izanagi and Izanami) created the world and gave birth to a sun goddess, Amaterasu, who is the ancestress of the Emperor. She is the principal deity. Her sister was Tsukiyomi, goddess of the Moon. The main shrine at Ise is dedicated to Amaterasu. Other deities include storm and thunder deities, rain gods, gods of the wind, earthquake gods, river gods, sea gods, gods of rocks and stones, and many more.

Many of the Japanese symbols are taken from family crests, known as *mons*, most of which are made up of simple lines frequently arranged in intertwining artistic patterns.

Tsuru, the Crane of Good Luck

Kame, the Tortoise of Longevity

Scythes

Fans

Scrolls

Forms

Gateway

The gateway to a Shinto shrine is known as a *torii*. The ends
of the horizontal bars are said to be reaching toward heaven.

$\mathfrak{S}$IKH

Sikhism was founded by Guru Nanak, in India, in the fifteenth century. It is a monotheistic religion with a "formless god." Sikhism teaches a need to meditate on the Divine Name *(Wahaguru)*. The believer should strive for union with the deity through hard work and by sharing what he has with others. Central to the Sikh faith is the concept of service; thus Sikhs are encouraged to overcome selfish desires. After Guru Nanak came nine other gurus, most of them remembered for their writings. The holy book containing the writings of the ten gurus is called the *Guru Granth Sahib*, and is written in the Punjabi language, in Gurmukhi script.

Nishan Sahib

The emblem on the Nishan Sahib, the Sikh flag, is made up of a double-edged sword, two scimitars, and a *quoit*, or circular throwing blade.

ᴄRAVELERS

Travelers include the *Romani* or *Roma* (Gypsies), Irish tinkers (who are quite separate and distinct from Gypsies), hobos, and other nomadic and homeless peoples.

The Roma originated in northern India, being driven out of that area by a succession of invading armies in the tenth and eleventh centuries. Thousands of these people moved westward and, over the centuries, dispersed across Europe, Asia, and eventually all around the world. By the fourteenth century they were in Rumania and Yugoslavia; by the beginning of the fifteenth century they had reached England. With their dark coloring and bright clothing, many believed them to be descendants of the ancient Egyptians and, in fact, came to call them *Egyptians*. This then was shortened to *Gyptians*, and, finally, to *Gypsies*.

From the start the Roma were constantly moving on; no country wanted to be overwhelmed by the itinerants. They were prosecuted, persecuted, banished, and constantly abused.

Yet they survived. They made their living as best they could, living by their wits and, for survival, taking advantage of the weaknesses of their persecutors. To help avoid persecution, the Roma would adopt the religion of the local people, outwardly practicing it while inwardly continuing their own Pagan beliefs.

The Irish tinkers were itinerant Travelers who already existed before the arrival of the true Roma. They were nomads who made a living by performing a variety of trades, including peddling, tin-smithing, and horse-trading. Their language is known as *Cant*, while the Roma language is *Romanes*. There has, however, been an adoption of various words, one into the other, over the years; Romanes words appear in Cant, and Cant words in Romanes.

There is often a blending of the signs and symbols used by Travelers since, for example, hobos have picked up a lot of the Gypsy sign language. These signs, often scrawled in chalk or scratched with a stone outside a dwelling, are left to advise others of the reception that might be expected at the house. The signs may be left for Gypsies selling wares, by hobos begging handouts, and/or by tinkers selling services.

Warning Signs

Owner has a gun

Dishonest person

Warning Signs *(continued)*

Dangerous dog

Unsafe

Be prepared to defend yourself

You will be beaten

Danger

Afraid

All right; Okay

Doubtful

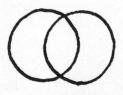

Don't give up

Cautionary Signs

Keep quiet

Well-guarded house

Dog

Halt

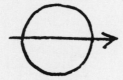

Go

Judge lives here

Kindhearted woman

Woman alone

Cautionary Signs *(continued)*

Gentleman

Officer

Jail

Information Signs

Telephone

Railroad

Trolley

You may camp here

Information Signs *(continued)*

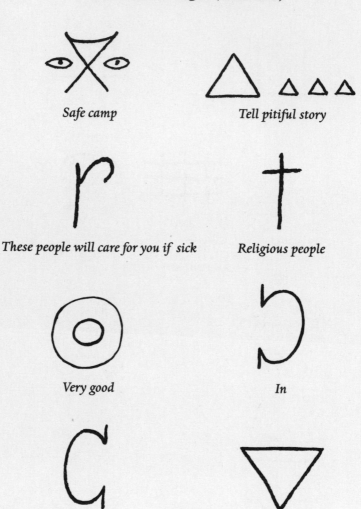

Safe camp

Tell pitiful story

These people will care for you if sick

Religious people

Very good

In

Out

Spoiled

Information Signs (*continued*)

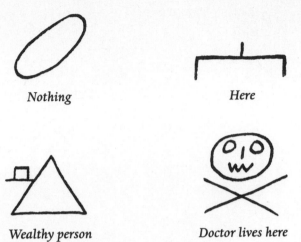

Nothing   *Here*

Wealthy person   *Doctor lives here*

Here are some other signs and symbols used by the Romani on talismans and magical items and as decoration:

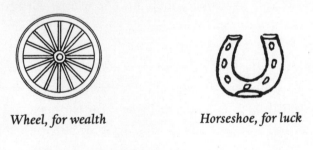

Wheel, for wealth   *Horseshoe, for luck*

Seven-pointed star, for long life and protection

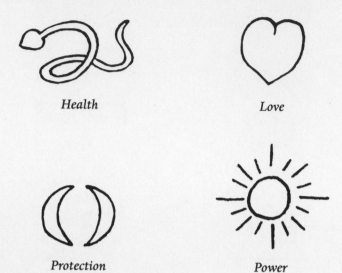

Health

Love

Protection

Power

Along with these actual marked signs, the Roma employ what is known as *patrin*. This is another form of sign language, usually used when traveling to indicate the path taken by a leading individual or group. At a crossroads, for example, a tuft of grass may be tied into a knot alongside the road taken. Stones may be moved to form a pattern, or simply an arrow, to indicate a direction. Branches, or the twigs of bushes, may be broken or bent to give an indication of where a forward group has gone, or other information such as the time of day that spot was passed. From the latter, the following group would know how far ahead the leading individual or group was likely to be.

Ⅴ̴OUDOUN

Voudoun is a polytheistic religion that was brought from Africa to the Caribbean by the slaves at the end of the seventeenth century. It originated in the kingdom of Dahomey, in West Africa. Spelled, variously, voodoo, voodoun, vodu, vodun, vaudou, etc., originally these were terms applied to deities in Dahomey.

In Voudoun it is believed that humans have a material body that is animated by a soul or spirit known as an *esprit* or a *gros-bon-ange*. This spirit lives on after death. The spirit can temporarily take possession of a living person if the spirit has developed to the point of becoming a *loa*, a divinity. Such possession usually takes place during a formal ritual.

In the early days of slavery, the Roman Catholic Church exerted heavy pressure to try to stamp out all vestiges of this Pagan religion. In order to stay alive, Voudoun disguised itself by associating Voudoun gods and goddesses, known as the loa, with the Catholic saints. To the Christian priests, local family altars appeared to be Catholic shrines honoring the saints; to the householders, they were purely Voudoun altars.

Seeing the power of the Church, the Voudoun followers adopted some of its liturgy, hoping thereby to gain some of its power. In Voudoun ceremonies, therefore, paternosters and Ave Marias can be heard, blending in with the native rituals.

The Voudoun loa are made up of a large number of deities mixed in with ancestral spirits. Certain of the loa, however, are especially important. These are referred to as the *Rada* deities; the others being the *Petro* deities. The Petro have acquired something of a bad reputation and are frequently associated with the darker side of Voudoun magic. The Rada deities are guardians offering protection, while the Petro are more stern and less forgiving. The Rada deities can, and do, punish those who do not give them proper honor, but they do not punish as severely as the Petro. Differences can be heard in the ritual drumming. Most of the Rada drumming and dancing is done *on* the beat while that for the Petro is done *off* beat.

The object of Voudoun rituals is to commune with one of the loa. There is closeness between the worshippers and their deities, such that the people believe they may speak directly to an individual god or goddess, albeit while the deity is possessing, or "riding," the body of another worshipper (the worshippers think of themselves as "horses" for the gods). To this end, a specific design is drawn on the ground to indicate, and draw, the desired loa. These designs are known as *vevers*.

Voudoun worship takes place in a sanctuary known as a *humfo*. These vary in size, but are simple buildings divided into rooms. The largest room, usually in the center, is known as the *peristyle*, and it is there that the major ceremonies are held. Some humfos have the peristyle as a separate building, often open at the sides with a roof supported by posts. It is often circular in plan with the main altar in the center, built around the center post or *poteau-mitan*. Leading off from the peristyle there may be a number of smaller altar areas. There is usually one room set aside for Erzulie, the "Aphrodite" of the loa. This room would contain a large brass bed, a dressing table with an ample selection of makeup and beauty aids, and a closet filled with beautiful clothes.

Much of the symbolism of Voudoun is found in the vevers drawn to attract the loa. Each is very specific for a particular male or female loa. The *mambo*, or priestess, will take a handful of cornmeal and allow it to trickle through her fingers, tracing a pattern on the ground. This is an intricate design and any error in its construction is taken as a bad omen. But seldom is an error made, and the mambo will trace the design with amazing rapidity. Here are some of the designs used:

Damballah-Wédo

Damballah-Wédo is a serpent deity and the major male loa. All trees are his resting place. Thursday is the day, and white the color, sacred to him. He does not speak, but whistles and hisses. He is regarded as the "ancient and venerable father" who is the source of all wisdom and the origin and essence of all life. His very presence brings peace.

Erzulie Fréda Dahomey

Erzulie Fréda Dahomey is the loa of dreams, love, and romance. All feminine things are a joy to her: makeup, jewelry, perfume, dresses, and also cake and champagne. Her colors are pink and blue. Erzulie always wears three wedding bands for her three husbands: Damballah, Ogoun, and Agwé.

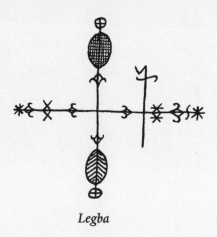

Legba

Legba is the "Loa of the Crossroads," the one who must be addressed first, for only he can open the gates for the spirits. Legba is a crippled old man who walks with a stick or a crutch, and has a pipe in his mouth and a sack over his shoulder. Originally he was both male and female, the initial procreative whole. The poteau-mitan—the central post around which the altar is built—is also known as the *poteau-Legba*. He is the guardian of the sacred gateway. Legba is linked to Carrefour, who, in turn, is linked to Ghédé, god of the dead.

Agwé-Taroyo

Agwé-Taroyo is the loa of the sea and all that is in it. Ceremonies to Agwé are frequently held at the seashore, where offerings are floated out to sea in small boats. He is a mulatto dressed in a naval officer's uniform, and he may carry a telescope under his arm. Blue and white are his colors. Agwé likes gunfire. He is a protector of seafarers.

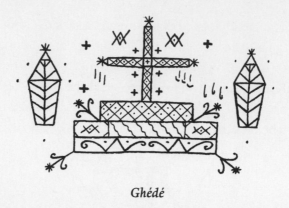

Ghédé

Ghédé is known as "Corpse and Phallus; King and Clown." His symbol is a cross. As Death, he is the keeper of the cemetery and is also known as Baron Cimitière and Baron Samedi. He is a very chthonic god, given to crude and lascivious words and actions and indulging in obscenities. He smokes a cigar and wears mourning clothes with a tall, black top hat. He also wears black-rimmed spectacles. Although a lover of death and sexuality, he is a great healer. Ghédé's wife is Maman Brigitte (or "Big Brigitte"). The Ghédé family is very prominent among the Voudoun loa.

Simbi

Simbi is the loa of the fresh-watered inland ponds, lakes, springs, and streams. He is the patron of rain. His symbol is a green snake, and his color is green. Simbi oversees the making of protective amulets and destructive magic charms known as *ouangas*. He shares connections with Damballah and with all the loa, both Rada and Petro.

Ogoun

Ogoun is also known as Ogu-Balindjo, a sky deity. His color is red, which is also the color of his eyes. Ogoun carries a saber. He is a warrior hero and a magician. He is a healer, with particular concern for children. Rum is a favorite of his.

Loco and Ayizan

Loco and Ayizan are the priest and priestess of the loa. Loco is "chief of Legba's escort." Ayizan protects against malevolent magic. Her symbol is a palm leaf, and her colors are white and silver. She never possesses anyone, since she presides over the rites.

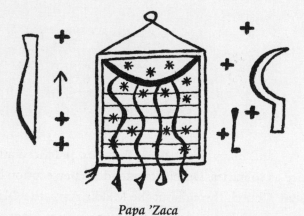

Papa 'Zaca

Papa 'Zaca is related to the Ghédés and is the god of agriculture. He is dressed in denim, like a country peasant, and carries a straw bag, a *macoute*. His color is blue, and corn meal and corn cakes are his offerings.

WITCHCRAFT

The word Witchcraft comes from the old Anglo-Saxon *Wicce-cræft*, meaning "the Craft of the Wise." The *wicce* (m. *wicca*) were the ones who were wise in that they had the knowledge of herbal lore and of healing, divination, and magic. This was part of a Pagan way of life that also incorporated a belief in deities of nature, and worship of those deities in the form of a god and a goddess.

Over many centuries—dating from pre-Christian times—form was given to the religion, with a priesthood and regular observance of seasonal rites. Groups remained autonomous, however, and many Witches, or Wiccans, practiced and still practice as solitaries. Despite tremendous persecution by the Christian Church throughout the Middle Ages, the Old Religion remained alive, and today Wiccans are once more able to practice openly.

There are many different traditions of modern Witchcraft. Certain symbols are shared by most traditions, if not all, while some symbols are peculiar to a particular tradition. Many traditions have a degree system for advancement. Let's start by looking at the signs for these degrees, as used by Gardnerian and similar groups, since so many Wiccan traditions are based on the original Gardnerian works.

First Degree

This is an inverted triangle. As with all of the degree signs, it would be drawn after the Witch's name when signing any document, though it is only used with the Wiccan name and not with the person's mundane name. The inverted triangle indicates the points that are kissed in the "Three-Fold" salute of the First Degree: breast, breast, genitals, and back to breast, to close the triangle. (In some traditions this takes the form: genitals, breast, breast, genitals.) Whatever pattern it follows, it forms an inverted triangle.

First Degree

The triangle is the triad, a design frequently associated with the female principle (the square is associated with the male principle). It ties in with the three aspects of the Goddess—Maiden, Mother, Crone—and concerns the Trinity. It was sacred to the ancient Egyptian Trinity of Isis, Osiris, and Horus; to the Indian Trinity, or Trimurti, of Brahma, Vishnu, and Shiva; and to the Greek Artemis, Selene, and Hecate. The Greek letter *D*, or *delta*, is a triangle and is described as "the letter of the vulva," and also as the "Holy Door." The Jewish tradition of triangular *hamantaschen* for Purim was almost certainly adopted from the ancient Egyptian custom of making triangular cakes for public rituals. In numerology, the number three, the number of the triangle, is ruled by Jupiter.

Second Degree

There is both a Three-Fold salute and a Five-Fold salute for the Second Degree. The Three-Fold follows a triangle, with its point at the top, and is mouth, breast, breast, mouth. In this normal position—with the point at the top—the triangle is also used as a symbol for fire, while inverted—with the point at the bottom—it is a symbol for water. (Upright with the tip cut off it symbolizes air; inverted and with the tip cut off it is a symbol for earth.)

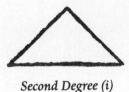

Second Degree (i)

There is also a Five-Fold salute for the Second Degree that is an inverted pentagram, or five-pointed star. The pattern of the salute again follows the pentagram shape: genitals, right breast, left hip, right hip, left breast, genitals.

Second Degree (ii)

Life Pentagram

A pentagram, formed by the seeds, is revealed when an apple is cut across. This is sometimes referred to by Roma, or Gypsies, as the "Star of Knowledge." The upright pentagram is associated with life. In many of the old *grimoires*, or books of magic, there is a picture of a man or a woman with legs spread and arms raised, with a pentagram superimposed on the body, symbolizing the life force.

Third Degree

This is a pentagram surmounted by an upright triangle. The pattern for the salute is mouth, breast, breast, mouth, genitals, right foot, left knee, right knee, left foot, genitals.

Third Degree

These salutes are given in various rituals, as acknowledgment of the degree of the Wiccan saluted. They sometimes play an important role in the ritual taking the Witch to the next higher degree. The Third-Degree salute, for example, plays an important role in that ritual of Third-Degree Initiation.

Athamé and Other Tools

The athamé (pronounced a-*tham*-ay) is the Witch's personal tool. The best athamé—the most powerful, in terms of energy—is that which has been made by the Witch himself or herself. If unable to construct one from scratch, then the very least the Witch should do is inscribe the handle, to put energies into the ritual tool. Different traditions have different sigils they use. Here are those sigils used in Gardnerian and similar traditions.

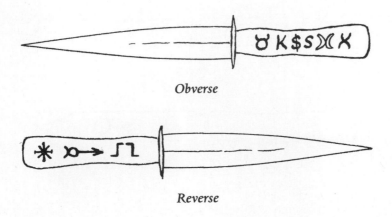

Obverse

Reverse

On the obverse, the first symbol represents the horned god and is followed by the letter *K*, the initial letter of *Kernunnos* (Latin for "the horned one"). Then come the sigils representing the scourge and the kiss, or salute. They are followed by the two crescent moons—waxing and waning—to represent the Goddess, and finally a symbol for the initial letter of her name. On the reverse of the handle is found a symbol for the eight-fold path (also said to represent the four greater and four lesser sabbats). Then comes a sign for the "power which is directed forth" in the working of magic. Finally there is a representation of two people, kneeling and facing one another—

the "perfect couple." In some traditions, after third-degree initiation the top lines are joined to make it one sigil.

In fact, all of these symbols are almost identical to the markings on the "knife with the black hilt" shown in the Ceremonial Magic grimoire *The Key of Solomon* (see also the chapter on Ceremonial Magic). This, then, is where Gardner got his symbols.

The Frosts' Church of Wicca teaches that their single-edged athamé should be made of aluminum, brass, or bronze. It is not marked on the handle but is etched on the blade, as follows:

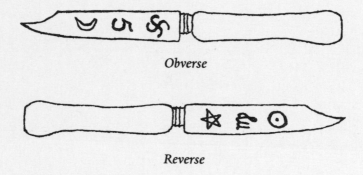

Obverse

Reverse

The swastika-like symbol is a double *S* for Spirit and Soul. The number is the owner's Birth Number, from numerology. It is followed by a moon. On the other side there is a pentagram and a sun with the owner's astrological birth symbol between them. (See also the chapter on astrology symbols.)

Some traditions also have sigils on other tools. In 1970 Paul Huson presented a book *(Mastering Witchcraft)* purportedly on Witchcraft, which was in fact a mixture of Wicca and Ceremonial Magic. He showed the markings on the athame as follows:

Huson Athame

It can be seen that these markings are similar to the Gardnerian ones, though with both sets placed on one side. In addition, without explaining the meanings, Huson gave markings
for the White-Handled Knife, in most traditions normally left
unmarked:

White-Handled Knife

Huson also gave Ceremonial Magical sigils for marking the
Wand, Goblet, Censer, and Candleholder:

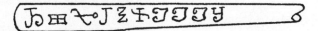

Wand

Goblet

Goblet Sigils

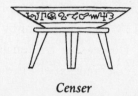

Censer

Candleholder

The Gardnerian Pentacle is a copper disc, about eight inches in diameter, which has a number of markings etched into it. These are the Third-Degree symbol, with First and Second on either side of it; symbols for the God and the Goddess; and the symbols for the Salute and the Scourge.

Pentacle

Book of Shadows

The Book of Shadows—a book that contains all the rites of Wicca—uses various symbols in the rituals, as written. A common one is ⊙, meaning "Circle." The **S** for Salute and the **$** for Scourge are also found there, as are the God and Goddess symbols: ♉ and ♍. Three-Fold, Five-Fold, and Eight-Fold salutes are shown as 5**S** (for example) or by the appropriate triangle or pentagram. Degrees are written as 1°, 2°, and 3°.

Some covens include mention of the elements and use the appropriate symbols.

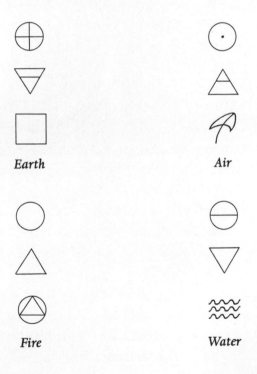

Earth   Air

Fire   Water

The spiral can be found in some books. This is an ancient symbol found at megalithic sites across Europe. In some places, such as at New Grange, in Ireland, there are double spirals, like two eyes. In other places, there can be found a triad of spirals. In some areas the spiral seems to represent a serpent, but in many places it has been associated with the idea of death and rebirth. The double spiral is sometimes seen as the breasts of the Mother Goddess.

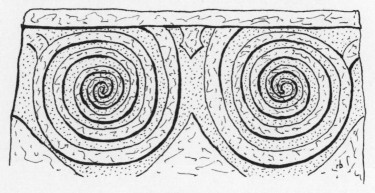

Double Spiral

In Wicca there is a spiral dance in which a line of people, one behind the other, dance into the center and then turn and re-trace their path outward. One name for this is the *Lufu* (from the Anglo-Saxon word for "love"). As the dancers turn to come out from the center, they lean across to kiss those going in. This was performed at the start of the sabbat meeting, especially when a large number of covens came together to celebrate.

Depending upon the Wiccan tradition, such objects as cauldrons, besoms (broomsticks), and even candles may be represented in the Book of Shadows with a symbol peculiar to that group.

Wicca Altar

Pennsylvania Dutch

In southeastern Pennsylvania, between the Delaware and Susquehanna Rivers, are found the European refugees from the countries bordering the Rhine River. They include Amish, Mennonites, Dutch Quakers, French Huguenots, Lutherans, Reformed, Moravians, and many other smaller groups. Although referred to as Pennsylvania "Dutch," most of them are German, the name being a corruption of *Deutsche*. These people have a belief in what they term *hexerie*, or "witchcraft." An extremely religious people, they are also very superstitious. For example, among their beliefs is that if a cross is painted on the handlebar of a door latch, it will prevent the devil from entering.

From such beliefs has grown an assortment of symbols known as *barn signs* or *hex signs*—decorative signs and symbols placed on the sides of barns and houses. These are not simply decorative but are utilitarian in that they are believed to cleanse evil, promote fertility, health, and happiness, and even start or stop rain. The signs are not used by the Amish and Mennonites—the plain sects—but by the Lutherans, Reformed, Moravians, and other church people.

Some hex signs have been used by the same family for generations and hence have become almost "coats of arms" for those families. Those in the know can see a particular sign on a barn and know immediately that one of the Miller family, for example, lives there.

Different symbols have become established in the signs over the years. Such objects as stars, of various types, are featured, generally for good luck.

Triple Star

Lucky Stars

Oak Leaves and Acorns, for strength of mind and body

Hearts, for love and romance

Rosettes, a basic hex sign ingredient

Distlefink   *Double Distlefink*

A distlefink is a goldfinch that ate thistle seed and used the thistle down for its nest. The distlefink was the good-luck bird of the early Pennsylvania Dutch settlers. It is sometimes displayed as a single bird and sometimes as a "double distlefink."

There were many other geometric patterns and signs. One early sign of protection was a form of the swastika. Many of the patterns were originally found tooled into the leather of family bibles, on illuminated manuscripts from the Ephrata Cloisters,[1] and on *taufscheine* (birth certificates).

The Witchcraft of the area is also called *braucherei* (healing without medicines), *powwow* (healing by words and motions), *hexa marrik,* and *gruttafoos* (marks placed to ward off evil). Some of the same superstitions and magical practices, though not the hex signs, are found in the Ozark region of Missouri and Arkansas.

1. A community of German Seventh-Day Baptists settled in Ephrata, Pennsylvania, in 1732 by Conrad Beissel.

OMENS

Omens are, in effect, nonwritten or nonprinted signs. They are indicators, or portents, of what is to come. Generally taken as warnings about future events, they are seldom considered as signs of a predetermined future, for, with the right actions, it is possible to circumvent what is indicated as being potentially threatening.

There are both personal omens and general omens. Personal ones give an indication, or warning, to a specific person, which is not necessarily applicable to anyone else. In this book, of course, we can look only at general omens. There are thousands upon thousands of these to be found around the world. I will look at some typical ones, concentrating on those common to the United States and Europe. Some deal with events, some with weather, some with health, and so on.

The Romans placed a lot of faith in omens, going so far as to seek them out in what they termed *augury*. There was even a college of augury where the augurs, the priests, studied and interpreted the signs of approval and disapproval presented by the gods. The office of augur was held for life. It was a position much sought after because of the political influence it had. It was bestowed only upon distinguished persons. Methods of augury varied from watching the movement of a flock of birds to studying the entrails from a sacrificed animal (the shape, color, alignment of the veins, etc., would all be taken into consideration), known as *extispicium.* When questioning the will of Jupiter, the augur would use a staff to mark out in the sky a ritual area known as a *templum,* much like a ritual circle, on the side or top of a hill. But he would also point, with the staff, to indicate the area of sky in which he expected the sign to appear. The augur would set up a small tent within the templum and would pray and sacrifice in anticipation, watched over by a magistrate. At midnight, the augur would expect to see the sign. He stood facing south, believing that all positive signs would appear to his left (east) and negative signs to his right (west). The Greeks took the opposite view, facing north, but still looking to the east as favorable and to the west as unfavorable.

Nature is seen as very orderly and rhythmic, so much so that whenever an anomaly is noticed it is taken as a sign of unexpected change and possible trouble. A good example is the observance of comets and even of eclipses. For centuries both such events have been taken as signs of possible approaching calamity. But even such minor events as animals behaving unnaturally, flowers blooming out of season, and birds changing their migratory patterns, have all been seen as omens. For oak trees to bud earlier than ash trees is an omen of a wet summer, while ashes budding first indicates a possible midsummer drought. To perform such a simple act as to pull the petals from a daisy, one at a time, can be taken as an omen of whether or not someone loves you. Omens may be found in the chance layout of tea leaves at the bottom of a cup, in coffee grounds, in the way dice fall, and in the spread of tarot cards. Any act of divination is, basically, the scrutiny of omens to find what is likely to happen in the future.

Animals

The appearance of a spotted dog, such as a Dalmatian, is regarded as a good sign. It is even better to see three white dogs together. If a dog is heard howling four times and then stops, it is an omen of coming death, and if a dog repeatedly rolls over in the same spot, it is symbolically measuring its master's or mistress' grave. If a strange dog comes to your house, it is an omen of good fortune to come. A dog laying in the doorway, facing inward, means someone is coming to visit; facing outward, someone will be leaving.

If a cat crosses your path, it may be good or bad, depending upon which way the cat is going. Yet here there is some confusion. Some say that if the cat appears from the right, it is a good sign, while others say that it must be moving *toward* the right to be a good sign. The same things are said for a rabbit crossing your path. It is also said that if a rabbit crosses your path and then turns and re-crosses, there is need for you to return home immediately. If a strange black cat turns up at your home, it is a good sign, but it is a bad sign if it then tries to stay permanently. If a cat repeatedly licks at a door, it is a sign of coming death for someone in that house. It is very good luck to see a white cat on the road, whether moving or sitting still.

To see a red-haired woman on a white horse is a very lucky omen, surpassed only by the sight of a red-haired woman riding a white mule. But to see horses running about and neighing is a sign of a nearby death. This is also signaled by seeing mules trying to mount each other near a house.

Shooting groundhogs is supposed to bring bad luck, though trapping them or hunting them with dogs is all right. To see an albino deer is a very bad omen. To shoot such an animal will bring death to the hunter. It is also considered bad luck to shoot any deer on a Sunday.

If you are on your way to visit someone and you encounter pigs in or beside the road, you will not be pleasantly greeted when you arrive at your destination.

Birds

If the first call of a cuckoo in the spring comes from the right, then it is a good omen. If from the left, then it is bad, announcing coming disaster. The sound of a screech owl is an omen of sickness and even death. If a person is already sick and hears an owl hoot, death will shortly follow. A chicken making a sound like a rooster's crow is a sign of death, and for a rooster to crow seven times is a similar omen.

If a whippoorwill sits on a house roof and gives its cry, someone in the house or in the immediate neighborhood will die within twenty-four hours. A crow flying low over a rooftop is an omen of illness to come, in the house. If the crow settles on the roof, there will be a death. When crows fly erratically or make sudden movements high in the air, it is a sign that there will be a very strong wind within the hour.

A barn in which barn swallows nest will never be struck by lightning. Barn swallows are generally considered lucky birds. To shoot one is to bring very bad luck. It is also considered bad luck to try to count the number of birds in a flock.

Insects

It is a very good sign if a swarm of bees lands on your flowers. Bees are traditionally bearers of good fortune. A bee buzzing around your head is a sign that there is a letter on its way to you with news of money or financial reward of some kind. You must always tell bees of a death in the family, otherwise you will have bad luck. Instead of telling them, you may simply turn their hive around to face the other way.

If a tiny red spider gets into your clothing, it is a sign that you will become rich. To be able to see your initials in a spider's web is to be especially blessed. If the web is at the entrance to a new house, you will be extremely happy living there. It is very bad luck to kill a spider, even accidentally. It is likewise bad luck to kill a cricket.

A praying mantis is a very fortunate sign. Never disturb one, or it will change any good luck to bad.

Weather

There are many signs of an approaching storm: crickets chirping loudly, large numbers of snails visible, flies and mosquitoes swarming, bees gathering close to their hives, or spiders leaving their shelters. Similarly, several hours ahead of a big storm, a hog will pile up leaves and brush. If a cat washes behind its ears or licks its fur against the grain, it's a sign of coming rain. When chickens and turkeys stand with their backs to the wind so that their feathers get ruffled, it is a sign of a coming storm.

When the hair in a horse's tail sticks out and appears bushy, it is a sign that a drought is coming to an end, and if a horse stops feeding and vigorously scratches itself on a tree or fence post, it is a sign of heavy rains to come. If cattle and horses refuse to drink during very dry weather, it is an omen of a coming cloudburst.

A deer lying down in the snow is a sign of another snowstorm within a few days. However, if a deer paws at the snow on the ground, as though to make a place to lie down, then there will be no more snow for at least a week. Butterflies or big wooly caterpillars seen late in the fall are an indication of approaching cold weather.

When and whether a groundhog sees its shadow and predicts the continuation of winter is a continuing debate. If it *is* done, and is of any real consequence, then many country folks claim that the time the groundhog would do this is February 14, not February 2.

A rainbow in the morning means that there will be a storm within twenty-four hours. A rainbow in the evening means clear weather ahead. When rabbits play about on a dusty road, there is soon going to be a rain shower. There will also be a shower if dogs eat grass. If ducks nest close to the water's edge, it will be a long, dry summer. If fish stick their noses out of the water a great deal, it means that a rainstorm is imminent. If it should rain while the sun is shining, the rain will not last long. Large raindrops indicate that it will be a shower of short duration, while small drops mean it will last a long time. When bees stay in their hive, it is a sign of rain on the way. When ants are exceptionally busy, it is also a sign of rain on the way.

When the sky of the rising sun is red, or if it is unusually clear, then rain can be expected during the coming day. But if the sunset is exceptionally red, there will be at least twenty-four hours of good weather. Lightning in the south indicates dry weather, while lightning anywhere else is an omen for wet weather. A falling star is a sign of illness to come, or even death.

The moon can be a good indicator of weather. A crescent moon, apparently lying on its back, is said to "hold in the water," so there will be no rain. But when the horns of the crescent moon seem to be tipped, then water can "run out" and rain is on its way. A ring around the moon is a sign of bad weather to come. In some areas of the Ozarks it is believed that the time the first snow falls can be an omen of the number of snowfalls that will come that winter: the number of days the moon is old equals the number of snowfalls to be expected. You should never look at the moon over your left shoulder. Look at the moon over your right shoulder for luck.

Objects and Events

The old superstition that to break a mirror will bring bad luck is recognized in many places. Usually it is believed that the bad luck will then stay around for as long as seven years. Walking under a ladder will also bring bad luck, though only a single incident of it. This superstition comes from the fact that to walk under a ladder angled against a wall is to break a triangle. Triangles are equated with the number three, and with the triad or the various Holy Trinities.

A sputtering coal in the fireplace indicates a coming quarrel in the house. If a clock should stop unexpectedly, it is a sign of a coming death. To meet an old woman (or a coyote, in the case of Native Americans) as you start out on a journey is a bad omen. So is accidentally putting on your shirt backwards. If you put on a shirt inside out, you have a bad day ahead of you. Tripping as you enter your house means you will receive bad news that day. Sweeping, with a broom, will bring bad luck if you do it before sunrise.

To have an itching palm is a sure sign that money is on its way. Some say that the right palm itching indicates money coming in, while the left palm is money going out. An itching or burning ear, or a sudden burst of sneezing, means that someone is talking about you. An itching nose means you will be kissed by a fool, though some say it means you will receive a love letter. To sneeze three times in succession is a sign of good luck coming. But then a further sneeze indicates a disappointment.

A knife dropped on the floor indicates that a male guest will arrive; a fork indicates a female. It is unlucky to cross two knives, and a knife should never be given as a gift—always take money for it, even if only a penny. If you drop a pair of scissors, gently step on them before picking them up, otherwise you will have a disappointment. If you drop a spoon, it means there will soon be a visitor (the direction in which the handle points indicates the direction from which the visitor will come).

If a baby is born as the tide flows (incoming), it is a propitious sign, while if a baby is born when the tide ebbs, it is a bad sign. A child born within twenty-four hours after a new moon will grow up to be very lucky and to have a long life. It is a very good omen if you spill your drink while making a toast. But if you drop your glass and it breaks, it is a sign of coming death to the one being toasted. If a picture should fall off a wall, it is an omen of death to come. Climbing in through a window is bad luck unless you climb out again through the same window.

ℬIBLIOGRAPHY

Introduction

Jung, Carl Gustav. *Psychology and Alchemy*. London: Routledge & Kegan Paul, 1953.

Alchemy

Albertus, Frater. *The Alchemist's Handbook*. New York: Samuel Weiser, 1974.

Constable, George, ed. *Secrets of the Alchemists*. Alexandria, Va.: Time-Life Books, 1990.

Eliade, Mircea. *The Forge and the Crucible: The Origin and Structure of Alchemy*. Translated from the French by Stephen Corrin. New York: Harper, 1971.

Gilchrist, Cherry. *Alchemy: The Great Work*. Wellingborough: Aquarian Press, 1978.

Haeffner, Mark. *Dictionary of Alchemy*. London: Aquarian Press, 1991.

Jung, Carl Gustav. *Psychology and Alchemy*. London: Routledge & Kegan Paul, 1953.

Klossowski de Rola, Stanislas. *Alchemy: The Secret Art*. New York: Thames and Hudson, 1973.

Multhauf, Robert P. *The Origins of Chemistry*. New York: Oldbourne, 1966.

Raleigh, Albert Sidney. *The Hermetic Art*. Chicago: Hermetic Publishing Company, 1919.

———. *The Philosophy of Alchemy*. Chicago: Hermetic Publishing Company, 1924.

Read, John. *Prelude to Chemistry*. London: G. Bell & Sons, Ltd., 1936.

Roob, Alexander. *Alchemy & Mysticism: The Hermetic Museum*. English translation by Shaun Whiteside. New York: Taschen, 1997.

Ruland, Martin. *A Lexicon of Alchemy*. Translated by A. E. White. New York: Samuel Weiser, 1964.

Taylor, Frank Sherwood. *The Alchemists*. New York: Collier Books, 1962.

Waite, Arthur Edward. *Lives of the Alchemystical Philosophers*. 1888. Reprint, N.Y.: Rudolf Steiner Publications, 1970.

Ancient Egypt

Aldred, Cyril. *The Egyptians*. London: Thames & Hudson, 1961.

Budge, Sir E. A. Wallis, ed. *The Book of the Dead*. New Hyde Park, N.Y.: University Books, 1960.

———. *Egyptian Language*. London: Routledge & Kegan Paul, 1970.

———. *Egyptian Magic*. London: K. Paul, Trench, Trübner & Co., 1899.

———. *Osiris and the Egyptian Resurrection*. New York: Dover Publications, 1973.

Cottrell, Leonard. *Life Under the Pharaohs*. London: Evans Bros., 1955.

Erman, Adolf. *The Ancient Egyptians*. Translated from the German by Aylward M. Blackman. New York: Harper & Row, 1966.

Rawlinson, George. *History of Ancient Egypt*. New York: Dodd, Mead & Co., 1880.

Wilkinson, Sir J. Gardner. *A Popular Account of the Ancient Egyptians*. New York: Crescent Books, 1988.

Astrology

George, Llewellyn. *The New A to Z Horoscope Maker and Delineator.* St. Paul, Minn.: Llewellyn Publications, 1970.

Lewi, Grant. *Heaven Knows What.* Garden City, N.Y.: Doubleday, Doran & Company, Inc., 1935.

Lewis, Ursula. *Chart Your Own Horoscope: For Beginner and Professional.* New York: Grosset & Dunlap, 1976.

MacNeice, Louis. *Astrology.* London: Aldus Books, 1964.

Parker, Derek and Julia. *The Compleat Astrologer.* New York: McGraw-Hill, 1971.

Australian Aboriginal

Elkin, A. P. *The Australian Aborigines.* New York: Doubleday, 1964.

Lawlor, Robert. *Voices of the First Day: Awakening in the Aboriginal Dreamtime.* Rochester, Vt.: Inner Traditions International, 1991.

Mountford, Charles P. *Art, Myth and Symbolism: Records of the American-Australian Scientific Expedition to Arnhem Land.* Melbourne University Press, 1956.

Aztec and Mayan

Miller, Mary, and Karl Taube. *The Gods and Symbols of Ancient Mexico and the Maya.* London: Thames & Hudson, 1993.

Spinden, Herbert J. *Ancient Civilizations of Mexico and Central America.* New York: American Museum Press, 1946.

Stuart, George E., and Gene S. Stuart. *The Mysterious Maya.* Washington D.C.: National Geographic Society, 1977.

Von Hagen, Victor W. *The Aztec: Man and Tribe.* New York: New American Library, 1958.

———. *World of the Maya.* New York: New American Library, 1960.

Buddhist

Bechert, H., and R. Gombrich. *The World of Buddhism*. London: Thames & Hudson, 1984.

Fields, Rick. *How the Swans Came to the Lake*. Boston, Mass.: Shambhala Publications, 1981.

Gach, Gary. *The Complete Idiot's Guide to Understanding Buddhism*. Indianapolis: Alpha, 2002.

Snelling, John. *The Elements of Buddhism*. Shaftesbury, Dorset: Element Books, 1990.

Celtic

Chadwick, Nora. *The Celts*. London: Penguin Books, 1970.

Laing, Lloyd. *Celtic Britain*. London: Paladin, 1981.

Norton-Taylor, Duncan. *The Celts*. New York: Time-Life Books, 1974.

Powell, T. G. E. *The Celts*. London: Praeger, 1958.

Ross, Anne. *Pagan Celtic Britain*. New York: Columbia University Press, 1967.

Ceremonial Magic

Barrett, Francis. *The Magus*. New Hyde Park, N.Y.: University Books, 1967.

Cicero, Chic, and Sandra Tabatha Cicero. *Secrets of a Golden Dawn Temple*. St. Paul, Minn.: Llewellyn Publications, 1992.

Denning, Melita, and Osborne Phillips. *The Magical Philosophy*. St. Paul, Minn.: Llewellyn Publications, 1974.

Gray, William. *Inner Traditions of Magic*. New York: Samuel Weiser, 1970.

Regardie, Israel. *The Golden Dawn*. River Falls, Wisc.: Hazel Hills, 1970.

Shah, Ikbal Ali, Sirdar. *Occultism: Its Theory and Practice*. New York: Rider, 1952.

Chinese

Blofeld, John, trans. *The I Ching: The Book of Change.* New York: Dutton, 1968.

Collins, Terah Kathryn. *The Western Guide to Feng Shui.* Carlsbad, Calif.: Hay House, 1996.

Kohn, Livia. *Early Chinese Mysticism.* Princeton, N.J.: Princeton University Press, 1992.

Yang, C. K. *Religion in Chinese Society.* Berkeley, Calif.: University of California Press, 1961.

Christian

Lewis, C. S. *Mere Christianity.* London: HarperCollins, 1995.

Palmer, Martin. *Living Christianity.* Shaftesbury, Dorset: Element Books, 1993.

Freemasonry

Mackey, Albert G. *Encyclopedia of Freemasonry and Kindred Sciences.* Revised and enlarged by Robert I. Clegg. Philadelphia, Pa.: L. H. Everts, 1887.

Pick, Fred L., and G. Norman Knight. *The Pocket History of Freemasonry.* London: Frederick Muller, 1953.

Plot, Robert. *The Natural History of Staffordshire.* 1646.

Wilmshurst, W. L. *The Meaning of Masonry.* New York: Bell, 1980.

Gnostic

Grant, R. M. *Gnosticism and Early Christianity.* New York: Harper & Row, 1966.

Hurtak, J. J., trans. *Pristis Sophia.* Pretoria: Academy of Future Sciences, 1999.

Jonas, H. *The Gnostic Religion.* Boston, Mass.: Beacon Press, 1963.

Greek and Roman

Adkins, Lesley, and Roy A. Adkins. *Dictionary of Roman Religion.* New York: Facts On File, 1996.

Barthell, Edward E., Jr. *Gods and Goddesses of Ancient Greece.* Coral Gables, Fla.: University of Miami Press, 1971.

Guirand, Félix. *Greek Mythology.* London: Paul Hamlyn, 1963.

Rose, H. J. *Religion in Greece and Rome.* New York: Harper & Row, 1959.

Hindu

Blavatsky, Helena P. *The Theosophical Glossary.* London: Theosophical Publishing Society, 1892.

Cross, Stephen. *Elements of Hinduism.* Shaftesbury, Dorset: Element Books, 1994.

Sharma, Arvind. *Hinduism For Our Times.* New York: Oxford University Press, 1996.

Islam

Brockelmann, Carl. *History of the Islamic People.* New York: Putnam, 1980.

Haeri, Fadhlalla. *The Elements of Islam.* Shaftesbury, Dorset: Element Books, 1990.

———. *Living Islam.* Shaftesbury, Dorset: Element Books, 1989.

Judaic

Butler, Walter E. *Magic and the Qabalah.* London: Aquarian Press, 1964.

Encausse, Gérard. *The Qabalah: Secret Tradition of the West.* Wellingborough: Thorsons, 1977.

Godwin, David. *Godwin's Cabalistic Encyclopedia.* St. Paul, Minn.: Llewellyn Publications, 1979.

Kenton, Warren. *Introduction to the Cabala.* New York: Samuel Weiser, 1972.

Regardie, Israel. *The Tree of Life: A Study in Magic.* New York: Samuel Weiser, 1969.

Magical Alphabets

Buckland, Raymond. *Buckland's Complete Book of Witchcraft.* St. Paul, Minn.: Llewellyn Publications, 1986.

Conway, David. *Magic: An Occult Primer.* New York: E. P. Dutton, 1972.

Encyclopedia Britannica. London: William Benton, 1964.

González-Wippler, Migene. *The Complete Book of Amulets & Talismans.* St. Paul, Minn.: Llewellyn Publications, 1991.

Mathers, S. L. MacGregor. *The Book of Sacred Magic of Abra-Melin the Mage.* Chicago, Ill.: The De Laurence Company, 1932.

Native American

Maxwell, James A., ed. *America's Fascinating Indian Heritage.* Pleasantville, N.Y.: Reader's Digest Association, 1978.

Owusu, Heike. *Symbols of Native America.* New York: Sterling Publishing, 1999.

Secakuku, Alph H. *Following the Sun and Moon: Hopi Kachina Tradition.* Flagstaff, Ariz.: Northland Publishing in cooperation with the Heard Museum, 1995.

Waters, Frank. *Book of the Hopi.* New York: Viking Press, 1963.

Norse

Branston, Brian. *Gods of the North.* London: Thames & Hudson, 1980.

Crossley-Holland, Kevin. *The Norse Myths.* New York: Pantheon Books, 1980.

Guerber, H. A. *Myths of Northern Lands.* New York: American Book Company, 1923.

Rosicrucian

Lewis, H. Spencer. *Rosicrucian Manual*. San Jose, Calif.: Supreme Grand Lodge of AMORC, 1959.

Lidstone, Ronald A. *Studies in Symbology*. Mokelumne Hill: Health Research, 1964.

Waite, Arthur Edward. *The Brotherhood of the Rosy Cross*. London: W. Rider & Son, Ltd., 1924.

Runic

Blum, Ralph H. *The Book of Runes*. New York: St. Martin's Press, 1982.

Blum, Ralph H., and Susan Loughan. *The Healing Runes*. New York: St. Martin's Press, 1995.

Elliott, Ralph W. V. *Runes: An Introduction*. Manchester: Manchester University Press, 1959.

Jackson, Nigel, and Silver RavenWolf. *The Rune Mysteries*. St. Paul, Minn.: Llewellyn Publications, 1996.

Shinto

Bocking, Brian. *A Popular Dictionary of Shinto*. London: Curzon Press, 1996.

Reader, Ian. *Religion in Contemporary Japan*. London: Macmillan, 1991.

Sikh

McLeod, W. H. *The Sikhs: History of Religion and Society*. New York: Columbia University Press, 1989.

Travelers

Buckland, Raymond. *Gypsy Witchcraft and Magic*. St. Paul, Minn.: Llewellyn Publications, 1998.

Fraser, Angus. *The Gypsies*. Oxford: Blackwell, 1992.

Gmelch, G. *The Irish Tinkers*. Menlo Park, Calif.: Waveland Press, 1977.

McDowell, Bart. *Gypsies: Wanderers of the World*. Washington, D. C.: National Geographic Society, 1970.

Voudoun

Deren, Maya. *Divine Horsemen: The Living Gods of Haiti*. London: Thames & Hudson, 1953.

McGregor, Pedro. *The Moon and Two Mountains*. London: Souvenir Press, 1966.

St. Clair, David. *Drum and Candle*. New York: Souvenir Press, 1971.

Tallant, Robert. *Voodoo In New Orleans*. New York: Macmillan, 1946.

Witchcraft

Buckland, Raymond. *Buckland's Complete Book of Witchcraft*. St. Paul, Minn.: Llewellyn Publications, 2002.

———. *Wicca For Life*. New York: Citadel, 2001.

———. *The Witch Book: Encyclopedia of Witchcraft, Wicca and Neo-paganism*. Canton: Visible Ink Press, 2002.

———. *Witchcraft from the Inside*. St. Paul, Minn.: Llewellyn Publications, 2001.

Campanelli, Pauline. *Ancient Ways*. St. Paul, Minn.: Llewellyn Publications, 1991.

Cunningham, Scott. *Living Wicca*. St. Paul, Minn.: Llewellyn Publications, 1993.

Huson, Paul. *Mastering Witchcraft*. New York: G. P. Putnam, 1970.

Omens

Buckland, Raymond. *The Fortune-Telling Book: Encyclopedia of Divination and Soothsaying*. Detroit: Visible Ink Press, 2003.

Gibson, Walter B., and Litzka R. Gibson. *The Complete Illustrated Book of the Psychic Sciences*. New York: Doubleday, 1966.

Leach, Maria, ed. *Funk & Wagnalls Standard Dictionary of Folklore, Mythology, and Legend*. San Francisco: Harper & Row, 1984.

Opie, Iona, and Moira Tatem, eds. *A Dictionary of Superstitions*. New York: Oxford University Press, 1990.

Randolph, Vance. *Ozark Superstitions*. New York: Columbia University Press, 1947.

LLEWELLYN ORDERING INFORMATION

Order Online:

Visit our website at www.llewellyn.com, select your books, and order
them on our secure server.

Order by Phone:

- Call toll-free within the U.S. at 1-877-NEW-WRLD
  (1-877-639-9753). Call toll-free within Canada at
  1-866-NEW-WRLD (1-866-639-9753)
- We accept VISA, MasterCard, and American Express

Order by Mail:

Send the full price of your order (MN residents add 7% sales tax) in
U.S. funds, plus postage & handling to:

> **Llewellyn Worldwide**
> **P.O. Box 64383, Dept. 0-7387-0234-x**
> **St. Paul, MN 55164-0383, U.S.A.**

Postage & Handling:

Standard (U.S., Mexico, & Canada). If your order is:
$49.99 and under, add $3.00
$50.00 and over, FREE STANDARD SHIPPING

AK, HI, PR: $15.00 for one book plus $1.00 for
each additional book.

International Orders (airmail only):
$16.00 for one book plus $3.00 for each additional book

Orders are processed within 2 business days.
Please allow for normal shipping time. Postage and handling rates subject to change.

ADVANCED CANDLE MAGICK

More Spells and Rituals for Every Purpose

RAY BUCKLAND

Seize control of your destiny with the simple but profound practice of *Advanced Candle Magick*. Ray Buckland's first book on candle magick—*Practical Candleburning Rituals*—explained the basic techniques of directing positive forces and "making things happen." In *Advanced Candle Magick*, you'll use advanced spells, preparatory work, visualization, and astrology to improve and enhance your results. Create a framework conducive to potent spellwork through the use of planetary hours, days of the week, herb and stone correspondences, and color symbolism. Create positive changes in your relationships, finances, health, and spirit when you devise your own powerful rituals based upon the sample spells presented in this book. Taking spellworking one step further, Ray Buckland gives you what you've been waiting for: *Advanced Candle Magick*.

1-56718-103-1, 280 pp., 5¼ x 8, illus.   **$12.95**

BUCKLAND'S COMPLETE BOOK OF WITCHCRAFT

RAYMOND BUCKLAND

Here is the most complete resource to the study and practice of modern, nondenominational Wicca. This is a lavishly illustrated, self-study course for the solitary or group. Included are rituals; exercises for developing psychic talents; information on all major "sects" of the Craft; sections on tools, beliefs, dreams, meditations, divination, herbal lore, healing, ritual clothing; and much, much more. This book unites theory and practice into a comprehensive course designed to help you develop into a practicing Witch, one of the "Wise Ones." It is written by Ray Buckland, a very famous and respected authority on Witchcraft who first came public with the Old Religion in the United States. Large format with workbook-type exercises, profusely illustrated and full of music and chants. Takes you from A to Z in the study of Witchcraft.

Never before has so much information on the Craft of the Wise been collected in one place. Traditionally, there are three degrees of advancement in most Wiccan traditions. When you have completed studying this book, you will be the equivalent of a Third-Degree Witch. Even those who have practiced Wicca for years find useful information in this book, and many covens are using this for their textbook. If you want to become a Witch, or if you merely want to find out what Witchcraft is really about, you will find no better book than this.

0-87542-050-8, 304 pp., 8½ x 11, illus.   **$17.95**
Also available in Spanish

BUCKLAND'S BOOK OF SPIRIT COMMUNICATIONS

Raymond Buckland

There has been a revival of spiritualism in recent years, with more and more people attempting to communicate with disembodied spirits via talking boards, seances, and other mediums.

Buckland's Book of Spirit Communications is for anyone who wishes to communicate with spirits, as well as for the less adventurous who simply want to satisfy their curiosity about the subject. Explore the nature of the spiritual body and learn how to prepare yourself to become a medium. Experience for yourself the trance state, clairvoyance, psychometry, table tipping, levitation, talking boards, automatic writing, spiritual photography, spiritual healing, distant healing, channeling, and development circles. Also learn how to avoid spiritual fraud.

0-7387-0399-0, 272 pp., 8 ½ x 11, illus. $17.95

To order, call 1-877-NEW-WRLD
Prices subject to change without notice

PRACTICAL CANDLEBURNING RITUALS

Spells & Rituals for Every Purpose

RAYMOND BUCKLAND

This trusted guidebook by popular author Raymond Buckland has introduced candle magick to more than 300,000 readers. From winning love to conquering fear, obtaining money to improving relationships, *Practical Candleburning Rituals* is filled with simple candle rites that get real results.

Newly updated and re-organized, this edition includes thirty-seven rituals—adapted for Christians and Pagans—that can be performed at home with readily available materials. No prior magickal knowledge is necessary. Diagrams and simple instructions make this candle magick primer an ideal practical guide for beginners.

0-87542-048-6, 264 pp., 5 ¾₆ x 8   **$9.95**